The Shelley-Byron Men:

Lost angels of a ruined paradise.

Portrait of Shelley by William Edward West

The Shelley-Byron Men

Lost angels of a ruined paradise

—From Adonais, line 88

John Lauritsen

Pagan Press

2017

The Shelley-Byron Men:
Lost angels of a ruined paradise
By John Lauritsen

Correspondence regarding this book can be sent to the author: john@paganpressbooks.com .

Pagan Press was founded in 1982 to "publish books of interest to the intelligent gay man." *Pagan* here denotes the culture of Western Classical Antiquity.

Printed on acid-free paper.

Library of Congress Control Number 2017901430

ISBN 978-0-943742-30-4 Hardcover

+ I. Shelley p. 27
II. Byron p. 47
III. Medwin p. 64
IV. Trelawny p. 72
V. Williams p. 76
VI Hogg p. 82
VII Peacock p. 87
VIII Don Leon p 90

CONTENTS

Illustrations

So, we'll go no more a roving
So late into the night,
Though the heart be still as loving,
And the moon be still as bright.

For the sword outwears its sheath,
And the soul wears out the breast,
And the heart must pause to breathe,
And love itself have rest.

Though the night was made for loving,
And the day returns too soon,
Yet we'll go no more a-roving
By the light of the moon.

—— Byron

Preface

This book originated from a talk, *Male Love in the Shelley-Byron Circle,* which I gave in 2002 to the New York City Gay History Reading Group. At the time I intended to make it into a full-length book, but one thing after another kept coming up, and the book ended up on the back burner. I kept acquiring more and more material, published four books and wrote several articles and book chapters on the Shelley-Byron circle, and I entered into a sometimes fraught relationship with the North American Society for the Study of Romanticism (NASSR). But the book seemed to recede further and further from publication.

Then one day I took another look at my old talk and realized that I already had a book, if not quite what I'd planned. I have expanded and re-written the talk, cannibalized some of my other writings, and relegated some material to appendices. Although I had originally intended a longer and more conventional book, I don't mind the brevity of this book. It is an overview, in which I try to show both forest and trees. In the past decade I have read all too many long and boring books where the authors are unable to say anything concisely. At any rate, there is much more to be done; and I hope that younger scholars will take up where I have left off.

In this book I aim to show that the Shelley-Byron men experienced and valued male love and were pioneers in trying to emancipate it. Under the sway of prejudice and superstition, their lives and works have been falsified by academics, literary critics, and biographers. As an independent scholar, I have no academic career to jeopardize by telling the truth.

Most of the research for this book was done in the 42nd Street library in New York City, in Widener library at Harvard, and in the Boston Athenaeum, where I did much of the writing.

John Lauritsen

Introduction

I should first define my terms and lay out my premises. The reader may not agree with them, but ought to know what they are.

I began studying "homosexuality" as an adolescent, clandestinely reading books in a small town Carnegie library in Nebraska. There wasn't much back then, two-thirds of a century ago, but the library did have Havelock Ellis's *Studies in the Psychology of Sex*, the Kinsey surveys, and Donald Webster Cory's *The Homosexual in America*. Even these gave me a historical perspective: I was not entirely alone.

In my freshman year at Harvard I used the much greater resources of Widener library to research the topic. My epiphany came from reading two books: John Addington Symonds's *A Problem in Greek Ethics* and Plato's *Symposium*. These works informed me that in Ancient Greece, the birthplace of Western Civilization, the love of male for male had been accepted as a part of life and granted a place of honor — the Greek gods themselves had male lovers. I saw that the prevailing laws and prejudices were wrong, not love and sex between males.

Beginning in 1960 I attended meetings of the Boston Mattachine Society, and later, after I'd moved to New York City, meetings of the homophile Westside Discussion Group.

I entered sexual politics in July of 1969, when I became one of the first members of the New York Gay Liberation Front (GLF). Although some of my ideas have changed since then, I have never ceased to be active, mostly as a writer and researcher.

My point in relating all this is that my ideas on male sexuality have been formed from many decades of experience and study. They may go against the prevailing paradigms, but are nevertheless grounded in history, anthropology, survey research, and animal studies. I conclude:

> Human males are powerfully attracted to other males, erotically and emotionally. When males have sex with each other, they are expressing an ordinary, healthy part of the sexual repertoire, a phylogenetic characteristic of our species. If a man has any libido at all, it has a homoerotic component, whether or not he is aware of it. The condemnation of male love is a theological phenomenon: the taboo on sex between males in the *Holiness Code of Leviticus* (ca. 500 BC).

Along with books related to the Shelley-Byron circle, the Bibliography has what I consider the best books for an understanding of male sexuality.

A few words about terminology: I'll occasionally use *gay* as being in some contexts the least awkward and even least anachronistic word, defining a gay man as one who acknowledges homoerotic desire in himself. (*Homosexual* is unacceptable for linguistic as well as philosophical reasons.) Although all the men in the Shelley-Byron circle had wives and children, they were nevertheless *gay*, if the term encompasses both the bisexual and the exclusively homosexual categories. Rictor Norton (1997) has demonstrated that by Byron's time, the words *gay* and *lesbian* were already used and understood in their current, homoerotic sense.

Therefore, the following definitions:

- A *gay* man has recognized and accepted his desire and capacity to love another man.

- A *straight* man has denied his homoerotic desires, consciously or unconsciously, or is unable to act on them.

Note that neither definition makes reference to women. Almost all gay men have had some amount of heterosexual experience, and most of the rest could, if necessary, rise to the occasion. (It's easy enough, if you've had practice with other guys — indeed, I suspect that gay men are less likely to be impotent with women than straight men are, but this goes too far afield.)

At any rate, *straight* is a completely negative term. It does not mean *heterosexual*, but simply *not gay*. Until some time in the mid-20th century, both *gay* and *straight* were underground words of a criminal subculture. Edwin Sutherland, in *The Professional Thief,* one of the classics of American sociology, shows how such words had meanings that were unknown to *straight* (law-abiding) people — and all active gay men were criminals then. Until recently, males who had sex with each other were punished by death or imprisonment, in accordance with laws based on the Levitical taboo.

I'll also use *camp,* a word that has been discussed often, but seldom well. I define camp as the unique sense of humor — and style and sensibility — of gay men. Camp combines elements of theatricality, irony, and hyperbole. At the heart of camp is a mockery of the situation in which we find ourselves — our predicament as gay men in a malevolent culture — and so camp includes a mockery of sex-roles, a mockery of taboos and conventions, a mockery of danger, and a mockery of condemnation.

The term *male love,* whose linguistic heritage goes back to classical antiquity, comprises sex, love and friendship.

The Initiated

p. 23

The Shelley-Byron men — Percy Bysshe Shelley; George Gordon, Lord Byron; Thomas Medwin; Edward John Trelawny; and Edward Ellerker Williams — were an elite. Shelley, Byron, and Trelawny came from upper-class backgrounds; the others, from at least the upper-middle class. Byron was rich, Shelley was heir to a fortune, while the others had adequate incomes. They were intelligent and well educated. Most of them were good-looking.

It will be apparent in the next chapter that they used coded language and references in their writings and correspondence, which presupposes a kind of "gay consciousness".

One set of their references reflects a belief that men who practise male love are superior to the "uninitiated", a word used by Byron. Shelley called his favored readers *sunetoi*, a Greek word that might be translated as "cognoscenti", "enlightened", "initiated", "discerning few", etc. Shelley's contempt for the "dull intelligence" of the uninitiated is expressed in unpublished lines from *Epipsychidion* (Appendix V).

It is significant that in Germany, the word *Vernünftige* (the "enlightened", "discerning", "rational") — a good translation for *sunetoi* — was a code word for gay:

> Platen did in 1834 publish a poem with the code word "*Vernünft'ge*" [=gay] that to the initiated was a declaration of homosexual self-consciousness and solidarity ["*Sollen namenlos uns länger,*" written January 31, 1823]. (From Warren Johansson's entry, "Platen-Hallermünd, August von", in the *Encyclopedia of Homosexuality,* [Dynes].)

The literature of Ancient Greece has many allusions to the superiority of male love, from Plato's *Symposium* to the Lucianic *Erotes* (mentioned in correspondence between two of Shelley's best friends, Thomas Love Peacock and Thomas Jefferson Hogg). In *Erotes*, a debate contest takes place between advocates of love for males and love for females. At the end, the judge says that both debaters have spoken well, but the prize goes to the lover of youths. He sums up:

> Marriage is a boon and a blessing to men when it meets with good fortune, while the love of boys, that pays court to the hallowed dues of friendship, I consider to be the privilege only of philosophy. Therefore all men should marry, but let only the wise be permitted to love boys, for perfect virtue grows least of all among women. (Loeb edition)

This conception, so far from the feminist political correctness of today, is expressed in the blunter Arabic saying:

> Males for recreation.
> Females for procreation

In his survey of sexual behavior among American males, Alfred Kinsey was able to find only one significant difference between those males whose behavior placed them towards the homosexual end of his continuum and those who were exclusively heterosexual: the gay men had a higher "sexual substrate" (or sex drive), which is a positive characteristic: a high sex drive correlates with good health, longevity, and intelligence. (Kinsey 1941, 1948, Tripp)

The sociobiologist, James D. Weinrich, has conducted a meta-analysis, which indicates that gay men have significantly higher IQs than straight men.

Now, if there is a homoerotic component to the libido of virtually all human males, and if the suppression of male love is the product of a theological taboo, then the question arises: why, in the face of potentially dire consequences, do some men violate the taboo? I suggest that taboo-violaters are more robust, braver, and more intelligent than the common herd. Of course, there are exceptions.

The Shelley-Byron Men

The main text needs no introduction, except to clarify a few points. I do not intend to *label* the Shelley-Byron men, to imply that they were set apart from other males by their sexuality. I sometimes characterize them as *gay* — describing their awareness, but not assigning them to a separate sexual category.

Academics and biographers strenuously resist acknowledging homoeroticism in the works and lives of canonized authors, obtusely demanding forensic evidence of specific homosexual acts. This kind of evidence will not be found here — although a good friend of Byron, William Bankes, found himself in criminal court on more than one occasion.

Actually, it's remarkable how much relevant evidence we do have. Consider the case of Oscar Wilde. There can be no doubt that he was actively gay, since he was convicted and imprisoned for "gross indecency" (sex with rent boys). However, there is less evidence of homoeroticism in his published writings than there is in those of the Shelley-Byron men. The same could be said for other writers, who were no strangers to male love, but who kept it out of their writings.

The Appendices

Appendix I contains two writings of Thomas Love Peacock, a good friend of Shelley and the executor of his will. Peacock is regarded as one of the best satirists in English. The first, an excerpt from his novel *Crotchet Castle* (1831) is a brilliant example of high camp and a blistering attack on sexual prudery. One notes in particular his somewhat disingenuous use of "Uranian", which became a favored name of pederastic poets later in the 19th century. Peacock and Shelley were the first in the English language (1818) to use the word "Uranian" (*OED*). The second passage is an excerpt from *Memoirs of Percy Bysshe Shelley* (1858), which is open to more than one interpretation. It indicates a self-censoring reticence to describe the private life of his departed friend.

Appendix II is Shelley's essay, *A Discourse on the Manners of the Antient [sic] Greeks Relative to The Subject of Love,* which was intended to accompany his translation of Plato's *Banquet* (or *Symposium*). If published during Shelley's lifetime, the *Discourse* would have been the first in English to discuss sex between males; and his translation, still the finest in English, would have been the first to present the genders correctly, making it clear that male love is the subject of Plato's most beautiful dialogue. Unfortunately, both *Discourse* and translation were first suppressed and then bowdlerized by Shelley's widow, Mary, and were not published complete until 1931, more than a century after they were written.

Appendix III contains two excerpts from the writings of Edward John Trelawny. First are passages from his quasi-autobiographical novel *Adventures of a Younger Son,* a neglected masterpiece of English Romanticism. Trelawny describes, with amazing candor, a love affair between himself at the age of seventeen and De Ruyter, an older man of twenty-nine. Trelawny's anguished parting from De Ruyter, knowing he will never see him again, is heart-rending.

The other excerpt is from Trelawny's *Records of Shelley, Byron, and the Author,* another neglected masterpiece. Three "castaways" — Shelley, Williams, and Trelawny — run into each other and decide to discuss their lives as exiles living in Italy. They are "three birds of the same feather", who had been hoved out of their nests and "denounced as Pariahs". Despite their pariah status, they find the strength and courage to carry on: "How we escaped from the ground-vermin, reptiles, and traps, and gained strength to take this long flight, we must now tell." Although Trelawny could not say so directly, these are three young gay men candidly confronting their own oppression.

Appendix IV is an excerpt from Thomas Jefferson Hogg's *The Life of Percy Bysshe Shelley*, a witty and loving tribute to his friend. Hogg's brilliant biography is one of the most enjoyable books I've ever read — sadly almost unknown today, even to students of English Romanticism.

Appendix V is an annotated gay reading of Shelley's poem, *Epipsychidion*, together with highly revealing passages that Shelley excluded from publication. These excluded passages leave no doubt that Shelley had male lovers. He had contempt for those in thrall to heterosexual monogamy, as well as contempt for those whose "dull intelligence" could not comprehend male love. The excluded passages touch upon many of the ideas that would later be used by those who strived to emancipate male love.

Appendix VI deals with a portrait of Shelley done by the American artist, William Edward West. I defend the authenticity of the portrait against a Shelley biographer, Newman Ivey White, who, against all evidence and reason, claimed that West was a liar and that the portrait was really of Leigh Hunt.

The Shelley-Byron Men
Lost angels of a ruined paradise

This essay is about two leading English Romantic poets — Percy Bysshe Shelley and George Gordon, Lord Byron (hereafter Byron) — and three of their friends, who lived close together in Italy during the first half of 1822. Despite the censorious efforts of friends and family, and the obtuseness of biographers, ample evidence survives to establish the importance of male love in their lives and works. They were ardent Hellenists, whose reference point for male love was the homoerotic ethos of Ancient Greece.

Male love occupied a place of honor in Ancient Greece and was at least accepted in Rome and the rest of pagan Europe. This changed radically in the 4th century AD, when Christianity became the state religion of the Roman Empire, bringing with it the Judaic taboo on sex between males (*Holiness Code of Leviticus, ca.* 500 BC). From this time forward, men who violated this taboo would suffer dishonor, imprisonment, torture, and death. Male love became a sin and a crime: sodomy, *peccatum illud horribile inter Christianos non nominandum* (the sin so horrible it must not be named among Christians). (Lauritsen 1998)

With the Renaissance — the rebirth of classical culture — homoerotic themes begin to appear in the works of Ariosto, Beccadelli, Marlowe, Michelangelo, Poliziano, and Shakespeare. The emancipation of male love came on the historical agenda in the 18th century, as the Enlightenment brought a secular viewpoint to questions of morality and extended free enquiry to the *peccatum mutum* (the mute or silent sin). In 1791 the French Constituent Assembly introduced legislation which left homosexual acts unpunished (a reform more than two centuries ahead of the United States), and in 1810 the *Code Napoléon* decreed that private consensual acts between adults were not subject to punishment. (Lauritsen 1998)

Histories of the early homosexual rights movement usually begin with the writings of Heinrich Hössli (1836) and Carl Heinrich Ulrichs (1864), although underground gay scholarship undoubtedly existed much earlier. I suggest that one such underground group centered around Byron and Shelley.

The scene is set in Geneva, late 1819 or early 1820, at the large country house of a Cornish baronet. Edward John Trelawny, an ex-sailor, meets three young men recently returned from India, and they become good friends. Two of them, Edward Ellerker Williams and Thomas Medwin, are lieutenants on half-pay, who had been in the 8th Dragoons. The third, George Jervoice (or Jervis) of the Madras Artillery, soon drops out of the story. Trelawny and Williams are in their late twenties, and Medwin a few years older. At the "pretty villa" where they are living, Medwin often turns conversations to his cousin, Percy Bysshe Shelley, who was living in Italy:

> Medwin was the chief medium that impressed us with a desire to know Shelley; he had known him from childhood; he talked of nothing but the inspired boy, his virtues and his sufferings, so that, irrespective of his genius, we all longed to know him. From all I could gather from him, Shelley lived as he wrote, the life of a true poet, loving solitude, but by no means a cynic. (Trelawny 1858)

Without saying so directly, Trelawny conveys the impression that three gay men are discussing another gay man.

A letter from Shelley in 1820 urges Medwin to join him in Italy, "the Paradise of exiles, the retreat of Pariahs", and Medwin does so. The two cousins, reunited after an absence of many years, collaborate intensely in writing poetry, translating Greek and German, and studying Arabic. Before long they are joined by Williams, together with his common-law wife, Jane — and later by Trelawny. The far more famous poet, Lord Byron, has moved his residence to be near Shelley. And so, at the beginning of 1822, the circle of men living close together in Italy comprises Shelley, Byron, Medwin, Williams, and Trelawny. What brought them together, and what did they have in common? Biographers have shied away from asking these and other pertinent questions.

Both Shelley and Byron considered themselves to be in exile. Shelley in particular was homesick and bitter that he was unable to return to England. Why could they not return to England? Why did they choose Italy? One very good reason might be the disparity between Italian and English sexual legislation: in England sex between males remained punishable by death until 1861, but in Italy it was legal, thanks to the *Code Napoléon*. In addition, gay men have traditionally gone to Italy for the boys: famous from time immemorial for their beauty, their amiability, and their discretion.

It is my contention that these five men — Byron, Shelley, Medwin, Williams, and Trelawny — along with Thomas Love Peacock and Thomas Jefferson Hogg in England — were drawn together by sexual affinities, that they discussed male love, and endeavored to liberate it.

I shall not attempt to demonstrate that all or any of them were *gay*, for three reasons: 1) the lack of satisfactory definitions, 2) the difficulty of proof, and 3) the fallacies of labelling. In a book on "outing" the authors state:

> The biographer who must sift the evidence for the sexual proclivities of a historic personality faces a

> challenging task. The subjects themselves almost always took great precautions to destroy or have their heirs and executors destroy any "incriminating"' evidence. Then their biographers bent over backwards to shield them from accusations of homosexuality. (Johansson & Percy)

Instead, I shall argue that male love represented an important part of their lives and works, with male love understood as comprising love, sex, and friendship. All of these men had wives, mistresses, and children — a fact which, popular misconceptions notwithstanding, has no bearing on whether or not they were attracted to other males.

With few exceptions, critics and biographers have cast a blind eye on this aspect of their lives. In addition, the waters have been muddied by a campaign of disinformation waged by Shelley's widow, Mary, and her daughter-in-law, Jane, Lady Shelley — a campaign described as "the fraudulent and mistaken efforts to turn the romantic, pagan Shelley, as Hogg, Peacock, and Trelawny knew him in the flesh, into a Victorian angel suitable for enshrinement among the gods of respectability and convention." (Smith)

These two women and their accomplices endeavored to transform Shelley's image from that of an infidel, rebel, and advocate of Free Love, into a Christ-like milksop. Jane Shelley set up shrines for visitation and

° Such a terrible loss!

worship, containing items of clothing, locks of hair, and other quasi-religious relics. She commissioned a life-sized statuary by Weekes, modeled on Italian Pietas, which depicts Shelley-as-Jesus expiring in the arms of Mary (thus fostering a double Mariolatry). It goes without saying that the fabricators of the Shelley legend did their best to eradicate every trace of homoeroticism from the poet's life.

Their efforts involved suppressing and bowdlerizing Shelley's writings, destroying pages from diaries, attacking writers who told the truth, and defaming the character of Shelley's first wife, Harriet (who died two years after Shelley abandoned her for Mary Godwin). The destruction of evidence, and the manufacture of lies, has been so extensive that, in the words of Robert M. Smith, "... no definitive biography of Shelley can now be written." (Smith) Even recent biographers continue to parrot and embellish myths and slanders that were created well over a century ago.

Not only Shelley's life received this treatment. Byron's Memoirs, upon which he had lovingly worked for years, were burned after his death,° as were the final cantos of his long poem, *Don Juan*. Trelawny's letters also were burned. Two volumes of Hogg's *Life of Shelley* disappeared, through the treachery of Lady Shelley. (Seymour) The men in the Shelley-Byron circle who survived long enough to challenge the Shelley legend — Medwin, Trelawny, Hogg, and Peacock — were attacked for having done so, and to this day are treated unfairly by almost all Shelley and Byron biographers.

Taking all of this into account — the falsification of evidence, the unreliability of biographies, and the masks which gay men were and are forced to wear — my approach will be to bypass biographers and examine the writings of these men directly for expressions of male love, beginning with Shelley. Since the field is vast, I'll assume some familiarity with Shelley and Byron, although I'll try to keep this to a minimum.

It is important to heed the principle laid down by Edward Carpenter, one of the great pioneers of gay liberation:

> Since the whole weight of herd-suggestion actively fosters and encourages the expression of all feelings of love towards the opposite sex and actively represses any patently homosexual expression, one clear indication of the latter is worth more as evidence than a dozen conventional signs of the former. (Carpenter 1925)

"Clear indications" of "homosexual expression" are found in their use of coded references to male love. Suffice a few examples: Shelley's reference to Shakespeare's sonnets in the deleted stanzas for *Epipsychidion;* his insistence that *Epipsychidion* be circulated only to the *sunetoi* (Appendix V); his reference to Antinoüs in his fragmentary short story, "The Colosseum"; his references to "Urania" and "Uranian" in *Adonais* — Byron's references in *Don Juan* to Virgil's *Second Eclogue* and to the "initiated", his use of the code word "Hyacinth" — Trelawny's quote from *Troilus and Cressida*, the Shakespeare play which most explicitly refers to a homosexual relationship (Appendix III.).

We should bear in mind that all of these men were British subjects, and that even into the fourth decade of the 19th century, males in their home country, including adolescent boys, were hanged for having sex with each other. Such Jew-based cruelty!

Therefore, when we encounter male love in their writings, even expressed obscurely or in hints, we should realize that this took courage. Even *camp*, or perhaps especially camp, was a form of defiance.

I. Percy Bysshe Shelley

> He who beholds the skies of Italy
> Sees ancient Rome reflected, sees beyond,
> Into more glorious Hellas, nurse of Gods
> And godlike men.
>
> (Walter Savage Landor, "Shelley")

Percy Bysshe Shelley was born in 1792 to a rich squire in Sussex. In appearance he was tall, slender, good-looking, and youthful. Even in the final year of his life, as he was approaching thirty, he looked like a teenager. He passionately expressed his love for other males, and they fell in love with him. He was fascinated with the idea of androgyny, and he discussed male love and homoeroticism in some of his writings.

Edward Carpenter was a great admirer of Shelley, and in 1925 broached his gayness. Modeling his own life after Shelley's, Carpenter advocated socialism, vegetarianism, and nude sunbathing. In 1879 or 1880 Carpenter paid a visit to Edward John Trelawny (1792-1881), Shelley's last surviving friend. Trelawny would then have been in his late eighties and Carpenter in his mid-thirties. Carpenter wrote: "It gave me a strange thrill on leaving (and he died soon after) to grasp the hand of one who had been so near to Shelley, and whose character undoubtedly had a great fascination for the poet." (Carpenter 1916)

As the author of *The Intermediate Sex* and *Intermediate Types among Primitive Folk*, Carpenter was keenly interested in the elements of androgyny in Shelley's personal appearance, psychology, and poetry, most notably in his poems, *The Witch of Atlas* (disapproved of by Mary) and *Epipsychidion*. Carpenter observed that Shelley's relations with women were unhappy, transitory or "up in the air" — whereas he "certainly attracted the devotion of his men friends ... and was capable of warm and faithful attachment to them." Carpenter comments that "while the love-interest occupies such a large part of the general field of Shelley's poetry, it occurs almost always in a very diffused and abstract form." The many female characters in his poetry seem "peculiarly epicene and sexless."

I would go even further: although Shelley was a feminist and seemed to require sisterly female companionship, although he was married twice and fathered several children, there is little evidence that he was erotically attracted to women. Both of his marriages were unhappy. Both came about through the initiative of the women.

In early October of 1814 Shelley wrote to his friend Thomas Jefferson Hogg:

> I saw the full extent of the calamity which my rash and heartless union with Harriet ... had produced. I felt as if a dead & living body had been linked together in loathsome & horrible communion. (Jones. vi. 402 and Fn.3)

This effusion refers to Shelley's first wife, Harriet: an intelligent, well bred, loving, beautiful woman, who at the time Shelley wrote this letter was only nineteen years of age. It is hard not to interpret it as abhorrence of female sexuality, and indeed, the sentiment is what one would expect from a gay man who is trapped in a heterosexual marriage. Not that Shelley shunned female companionship — on the contrary, he sought it out and was particularly obsessed with tutoring girls and having female friends who to him would be sisters.

In the summer of 1814 Shelley left Harriet and fled to the Continent with Mary Godwin and her stepsister, Jane (later Claire) Clairmont. Mainstream Shelley biographers have assumed that Shelley was so overwhelmed with love for Mary that he impetuously eloped with her. But if so, why on earth did he take along her stepsister Jane for the trip? My own hypothesis is that Mary knew she was pregnant, that Shelley took her to the Continent to have the baby there, and that Jane went along to help care for Mary.

Another hypothesis is that Mary, raised in a radical household, had led Shelley to believe that she (and Jane) would be sympathetic to and understanding of his homoerotic desires. Mary's own lesbianism manifested itself after the death of Shelley. (Seymour)

Harriet Shelley died, allegedly a suicide, in late 1816, two years after Shelley abandoned her. Despite Shelley's principled opposition to marriage and his desire to respect the memory of Harriet, he was then coerced into marriage with Mary Godwin, who threatened suicide. (St. Clair 1989) Shelley's marriage to Mary, a cold and querulous woman, was not happy; for the last two years of his life he slept on the sofa and spent as little time as possible in her company.

If Shelley had one great love in his life, it was his dear friend Thomas Jefferson Hogg, who was expelled from Oxford with him, when they were both eighteen, over a pamphlet they had written together, *The Necessity of Atheism*. They lived together in London briefly, until they were separated by their families. According to Trelawny, Hogg's love for Shelley was "the one bit of romance in his life". Nowhere in Shelley's writings does one find such passion as in the letters addressed to Hogg:

> "You have chosen me, and we are inseparable" ... "Are you not he whom I love...?" ... "If I thought we were to be long parted, I should be wretchedly miserable — half mad!" ... "Will you come; will you share my fortunes, enter into my schemes, love me as I love you, be inseparable, as once I fondly hoped we were?" ... "Oh! how I have loved you! I was even ashamed to tell you how!" ... "Why did I leave you? I have never doubted you — you, the brother of my soul, the object of my vivid interest; the theme of my impassioned panegyric." (Hogg, Holmes 1974)

Hogg's reminiscences of Shelley, written thirty-six years after his death, are a loving tribute, and include numerous hints as to male love. (See section below under Hogg.)

The last love of Shelley's life was Edward Ellerker Williams, with whom he died. The two were "inseparable companions" for the final year of their lives. (See section below under Williams.)

Let us now examine Shelley's works, beginning with his translations. "Shelley was a translator of extraordinary range and versatility, whose acquaintance with European literature makes most English poets between Dryden and Eliot look provincial." (Webb) He had a penchant for translating works with homoerotic content, including elegies of Bion and Moschus and epigrams of Plato. To illustrate the conflicts Shelley faced, let's look at his translation of the (pseudo) Plato epigram, "Kissing Agathon":

> Kissing Agathon, together
> With the kiss, my spirit was
> Upon my lips and there I kept it —
> For the poor thing had come thither
> As if it were departing.

The problem here is that both Plato and Agathon are males, kissing each other in an amorous context. Shelley was well aware that this could not be done in 19th century England, and so, in his third revision he reluctantly changed "Kissing Agathon" to "Kissing Helena". (Webb) It is the ridiculous "Kissing Helena" version that appears in the Oxford edition of Shelley's *Poetical Works.*

Another (pseudo) Plato epigram expresses love and mourning for the boy, Aster, whose name in Greek means "star". Shelley rendered it as follows:

To Aster

Thou wert the morning star among the living,
Ere thy fair light had fled —
Now, having died, thou art as Hesperus, giving
New splendour to the dead.

Here only the title needed to undergo a sex change: the masculine name Aster became the feminine name Stella.

In 2001 I published one of Shelley's greatest, though least known, compositions: his translation of Plato's great Dialogue on Eros, *The Banquet* (or *Symposium*). This translation is not only incomparably the best in English, it is a masterpiece in its own right. But despite its excellence, the translation was first suppressed and then bowdlerized for well over a century. The Victorians could not countenance male love, which lies at the heart of the dialogue.

Shelley began translating *The Banquet* during the summer of 1818, when he was twenty-six years old. Working as though possessed by a Platonic Daemon, he finished the translation in ten days.

Shelley had lived with the dialogue for many years. While still a schoolboy at Eton, he was introduced to it by his mentor, Dr. James Lind ("that divine old man"), about whom he always spoke with reverence. Why did Dr. Lind introduce Shelley to this particular dialogue? Perhaps it was to inform his teenaged *protégé,* by means of the *Symposium,* that male love is a part of human nature, which had been highly esteemed by the Greeks. The significance of Dr. Lind's tutelage can be gauged through comparison with an event that occurred several decades later. In the 1850s, another English schoolboy, John Addington Symonds, read the *Symposium* for the first time. Alone in his room at Harrow, he experienced the great epiphany of his life:

> Harrow vanished into unreality. I had touched solid ground. I had obtained the sanction of the love which had been ruling me from childhood. Here was the poetry, the philosophy of my own enthusiasm for male beauty, expressed with all the magic of unrivalled style. And, what was more, I now became aware that the Greek race — the actual historical Greeks of antiquity — treated this love seriously, invested it with moral charm, endowed it with sublimity. (Symonds 1984)

Shelley then wrote an introductory essay to help his wife Mary understand "the manners and feelings of the

Athenians" (and also, presumably, his own). This essay, *A Discourse on the Manners of the Antient [sic] Greeks Relative to the Subject of Love*, is only the second in English (after an unpublished 1785 essay by Jeremy Bentham) to address male-to-male sexuality. (Crompton 1985)

The first part of Shelley's essay is an eloquent expression of Hellenism. It begins: "The period which intervened between the birth of Pericles and the death of Aristotle, is undoubtedly, whether considered in itself or with reference to the effects which it has produced upon the subsequent destinies of civilised man, the most memorable in the history of the world." For several pages, he describes the Greek miracle, in the realms of art, poetry, drama, philosophy, and science. (Plato 2001) When Shelley comes to his main topic, he ponders male love in Ancient Greece and its condemnation in his own time. He touches upon religion, the role of women, the beauty of Greek youths, and sexual ethics. (See Appendix II. Shelley: *Discourse on the Manners of the Antient Greeks.*)

At any rate, Shelley doubted that he could publish either translation or essay in the foreseeable future, although he showed them to his friends. Four years later, in July 1822, just short of his thirtieth birthday, he drowned in a boating accident. Eighteen years later his widow Mary, aided by Leigh Hunt, published the translation, but in a highly bowdlerized form: they changed "love" to "friendship", "his beloved" to "the other", "men" to "human beings", and so on; they truncated offending passages and entire episodes. This travesty was the only version the world knew until 1931, when translation and essay were finally published in their entirety — in a private edition of only 100 copies.

In 1818, the same year he translated the *Symposium,* Shelley wrote an essay, *On Love,* which contains a revealing passage;

> If we reason, we would be understood; if we imagine, we would that the airy children of our brain were born anew within another's; if we feel, we would that another's nerves should vibrate to our own, that the beams of their eyes should kindle at once and mix and melt into our own, that lips of motionless ice should not reply to lips quivering and burning with the heart's best blood. This is Love. This is the bond and the sanction which connects not only man with man but with everything which exists. We are born into the world, and there is something within us, which from the instant that we live, more and more thirsts after its likeness. [1]

[1] For a discussion of the essay, with a collation of all the variants, see *Shelley and his Circle: 1773-1822,* volume VI, edited by Donald H. Reiman, 1973

• actually plural

Shelley conceives of love as connecting "man with man" — something within us, which"more and more thirsts after its likeness" — an attraction of similars.

Thomas Medwin, Shelley's cousin and his first biographer, published *On Love* in his 1833 *Memoir of Percy Bysshe Shelley*. But Medwin flinched at the homoeroticism in this passage and made two highly revealing changes. First, Medwin changed a key pronoun from neuter (their) to feminine (her), rendering the phrase thus: "...that the beams of *her* eyes should kindle at once, and mix and melt into our own...." Second, he changed the phrase about *"man with man"* to *"the two sexes"*. This point is important: the homoeroticism of the passage is real (not merely a Freudian interpretation) and sufficiently obvious that Medwin felt obliged to bowdlerize it. And Medwin did know that his cousin was gay

In the fall of 1818 Shelley paid a visit to Byron in Venice, renewing their friendship after a hiatus of two years. Delighted with each other's company, they talked nonstop, from three in the afternoon until five the next morning. For days the two of them talked, dined, rode horseback, and travelled in gondolas together. Out of these experiences came *Julian and Maddalo*, one of Shelley's finest long poems, a highly autobiographical and problematic work. There are three main characters in the poem: Julian, Maddalo, and the "Maniac". Julian is Shelley, and Count Maddalo is Lord

Byron, but who or what is the Maniac? In his introduction to the poem, Shelley writes:

> Of the Maniac I can give no information. He seems, by his own account, to have been disappointed in love. He was evidently a very cultivated and amiable person when in his right senses. *His story, told at length, might be like many other stories of the same kind.* (Emphasis added.)

This is a very great, under-appreciated, and misinterpreted poem. Its deeper meaning can best be appreciated by knowledgeable gay men (the "discerning few"), who can apprehend the coded references, and who can respond to the poem from their own experience. For them it is a beautiful and moving expression of alienation and undeserved suffering. A heterosexual red herring involving a "lady" is thrown in, but the references to her serve no purpose other than mystification. Shelley himself slyly indicates that the "lady" should not be taken seriously.

I suggest interpreting it under two premises: 1) Julian (Shelley) and Maddalo (Byron) are gay men, which indeed they were, and 2) Shelley has employed gender trickery, which indeed he did elsewhere. By changing "lady" to "lad" (two occurrences) and feminine to masculine pronouns (ten occurrences), the poem makes sense.

At home in Count Maddalo's palazzo in the evening, Maddalo and Julian decide to camp a bit less and have a serious talk about something they find difficult to discuss:

> Our talk grew somewhat serious, as may be
> As mocks itself, because it cannot scorn
> The thoughts it would extinguish: — 'twas forlorn,
> Yet pleasing, such as once, so poets tell,
> The devils held within the dales of Hell....

Julian and Maddalo discuss religion and philosophy until late in the night, and the next day they sail to "the island where the madhouse stands" to visit the Maniac, who is known to Maddalo. They listen to his long soliloquy, in which the references to male love are clear and unmistakable. The Maniac speaks of having to "wear this mask of falsehood even to those/ Who are most dear." He is bound to silence: "And not to speak my grief — O, not to dare/To give a human voice to my despair." He refers to "deeds too dreadful for a name", which invokes the "unnameable sin" ("*peccatum illud horrible inter christianos non nominandum*") — which Lord Alfred Douglas later in the century would term "the love that dare not speak its name").

In the following passage, the Maniac touches on *the love that is friendship*:

O Thou, my spirit's mate
Who, for thou art compassionate and wise,
Wouldst pity me from thy most gentle eyes
If this sad writing thou shouldst ever see —
My secret groans must be unheard by thee,
Thou wouldst weep tears bitter as blood to know
Thy lost friend's incommunicable woe.

Note "spirit's mate" — a concept, the soul mate, which will be discussed with regard to the later poem, *Epipsychidion.*

In the following passage the maniac associates his form of love with the dungeon, shame, and the scaffold:

Heap on me soon, O grave, thy welcome dust!
Till then the dungeon may demand its prey,
And Poverty and Shame may meet and say —
Halting beside me on the public way —
"That love-devoted youth is ours — let's sit
Beside him — he may live some six months yet."
Or the red scaffold, as our country bends,
May ask some willing victim....

Shame, which Shelley has capitalized, is a gay code word which surfaced towards the end of the 19th century, most famously in the poems of Lord Alfred Douglas, "Two Loves" and "In Praise of Shame" (McKenna). The "red scaffold" and "our country" can only refer to England, where men and boys were still being hanged for making love to each other. What the Maniac personifies, then, is the suffering of gay men, who are unjustly despised and persecuted. He is a literary cousin of the *Frankenstein* Monster (discussed below).

Shelley's long poem, *Adonais* is an elegy, in Spenserian stanzas, for John Keats. It is also an elegy for gay men, martyred for loving each other. Not only does *Adonais* have coded references to male love ("To Phoebus was not Hyacinth so dear", "Urania"...), but at the very head of Shelley's introduction to the poem is a quotation in Greek of the Aster epitaph attributed to Plato, discussed above; this is a clear hint, for those who can read Greek, that the poem is about male love.

The subtitle for this book comes an *Adonais* stanza:

> And one with trembling hands clasps his cold head,
> And fans him with her moonlight wings, and cries;
> "Our love, our hope, our sorrow, is not dead;
> See, on the silken fringe of his faint eyes,
> Like dew upon a sleeping flower, there lies
> A tear some Dream has loosened from his brain."
> Lost Angel of a ruined Paradise!
> She knew not 'twas her own; as with no stain
> She faded, like a cloud which had outwept its rain.

In my interpretation, "Lost Angel of a ruined Paradise!" speaks to gay men, who are *lost angels*. The *paradise* is

Ancient Greece, where male love was free and honored — *ruined* by Judeo-Christian superstition.

Keats is outside the scope of this book. I hope that future scholars will finally do justice to Keats's love life and to *Adonais*. Whether or not Keats truly loved Fanny Brawne, the most enduring relationships of his life were with other men.

The last love of Shelley's life, his inseparable companion for the last one-and-a-half years of their lives, was the handsome and sensitive Edward Ellerker Williams, the same age as himself. Their relationship is charmingly depicted in *The Boat on the Serchio*, in which "Melchior" and "Lionel" represent Shelley and Williams, and the boat symbolizes their relationship. (More on this poem in the Williams section.)

In 1822 Shelley and Williams died in a boating accident, together with "a smart sailor lad" named Charles Vivian. (Trelawny 1858) Shortly before this Shelley had written an epitaph expressing his desire to be united with Williams, both in life and after death:

> They were two friends, whose life was undivided.
> So let them mingle. Sweetly they had glided
> Under the grave. Let not their dust be parted,
> For their two hearts in life were single-hearted.
>
> (Medwin 1847/1913)

It is my belief that, after their deaths, the ashes of Shelley and Williams were mixed together by the surviving men in the Shelley-Byron circle. (More below under Williams.)

The late poem *Epipsychidion* is particularly interesting for some additional lines, which were found and printed in 1903. Never intended for publication, they indicate that disguised male love is a theme of the poem and that heterosexual red herrings (akin to "Helena" and "Stella") have been employed. In a letter to his publisher, Charles Ollier, Shelley insisted the poem be published in strict anonymity, in an edition of only 100 copies: "It is to be published simply for the esoteric few." The reason for this secrecy, according to his biographer Richard Holmes is that "Epipsychidion is the most nakedly autobiographical poem he ever wrote."

In the passages below, "friend" and "mistress" are counterparts, meaning male and female lovers respectively. Note Shelley's reference to Shakespeare's sonnets and his contempt for the "dull intelligence" of those readers who are not among his *sunetoi*:

> Here, my dear friend, is a new book for you
> I have already dedicated two
> To other friends, one female and one male, —
> What you are, is a thing that I must veil;
> What can this be to those who praise or rail?
> I never was attached to that great sect

Whose doctrine is that each one should select
Out of the world a mistress or a friend,
And all the rest, though fair and wise, commend
To cold oblivion....

If any should be curious to discover
Whether to you I am a friend or lover,
Let them read Shakespeare's sonnets, taking thence
A whetstone for their dull intelligence....

G. Wilson Knight (1957) regarded the final four lines above as sufficient to say that Shelley was bisexual.

James A. Notopoulos interprets *Epipsychidion,* in the context of Shelley's other writings, as "soul of my soul" or "soul mate". Shelley took the concept from the speech of Aristophanes in Plato's *Symposium* (Plato 2001), in which lovers are "two incomplete parts of a pristine whole, which, after being separated by Apollo, have been forever seeking their counterpart soul mates." It should be clear that "spirit's mate" from *Julian and Maddalo* perfectly fits Shelley's conception of *Epipsychidion.* I suggest that both poems are concerned with the love of males for their male soul mates.

Epipsychidion is a cryptic poem, a *poème à clef.* Critics have speculated whether Mary Shelley is symbolized by "moon", Claire Clairmont by "comet", and so on. Shelley's dedication reads: "Verses addressed to the noble and unfortunate Lady, Emilia V————, now imprisoned in the convent of ———————". This refers to Countess Emilia Viviani, a young woman residing in the Convent of St. Anna, whom Shelley visited a few times and with whom he corresponded briefly. Although many lines of *Epipsychidion* appear to be addressed to "Emilia", this may be a red herring. There is no good evidence that Shelley was infatuated with Emilia — never once did he visit her without being chaperoned by his wife and/or Claire Clairmont.

After 406 cryptic lines, with occasional appeals to "Emilia", the poem suddenly shifts gears with a line break and an appeal to "Emily". The section that follows, addressed to "Emily" rather than "Emilia", is over two hundred lines of beautiful and erotic poetry. I propose that "Emily" is not a variant of "Emilia" but rather the nickname of Edward Ellerker Williams — Shelley's beloved companion. (The men in the Shelley-Byron circle did use feminine nicknames for each other, for example, "Polly" for Dr. John Polidori.) Shelley and Williams met in early January 1821, over a month before the *Epipsychidion* manuscript was sent to the printer. These concluding lines are far more congruous with Edward=Emily than with Emilia. In my imagination, Shelley fell head over heels in love with Williams and concluded *Epipsychidion* in a burst of inspiration.

Throughout *Epipsychidion* are references to sailing, which Shelley and Williams enjoyed from the time they met until the time they died together on the water, a year and a half later — references to the mutual attraction of equals or similars — references to soul mates, the myth of Aristophanes. The concluding section is a world, a sensibility of male love, and no other kind.

For an annotated version of the final lines of *Epipsychidion* see Appendix V.

Powerful expressions of male love are found in the novel *Frankenstein,* which was published anonymously in 1818. That this was not recognized long ago is due to the false belief that Mary Shelley, a hack writer at best, was the author — a belief fostered by Mary and her father, William Godwin, and by feminists who shamelessly tout her as a major writer. Mary did do the clerical work and perhaps a trivial amount of the writing, but the basic conception, the autobiographical elements, the imagination, and the splendid prose passages are unmistakably the work of Shelley himself.

Frankenstein is not just a scary story, not just a gothic novel, but a novel of ideas, written in poetically powerful prose. It is a moral allegory, about the evil effects of intolerance, both to its victims and to society at large. Thwarted male love and the undeserved suffering of gay men are major themes of *Frankenstein.* (Lauritsen 2007, Rieger, Zimmerman)

Let us turn now to the second major poet, Byron.

II. Byron

Biographers and critics, with very few exceptions, have refused to acknowledge homoeroticism in the life and works of Shelley. This is no longer the case with Byron, whose sexual predilection for males was known in gay circles at least as early as 1821, when it was alluded to in a Swiss publication. (Hirschfeld) In his magnum opus, Magnus Hirschfeld includes Byron in his list of famous homosexuals, as a bisexual. On the whole, Byron biographers have tended to downplay or ignore his attraction to males.

In researching a three-volume biography of Byron (1957), Leslie A. Marchand was given access to the Byron archives of publisher John Murray, the largest in the world, but only on the condition that he not allude to Byron's bisexuality. Marchand partially rectified his omissions in a later, single-volume work (1970), which disclosed that Byron had belonged to a gay circle at Cambridge, whose members used coded language among themselves.

G. Wilson Knight (1957) examined Byron's marriage, Lady Byron's desertion, and the subsequent scandal. He addressed the incest hypothesis — that Byron had an "illicit relationship with his half-sister Augusta Leigh" — and dismissed it as the primary reason for the separation: "There is good reason to suppose that this incest-motif has been all the time, whether or not there be truth behind it, playing the part of a peculiarly effective red herring." Rather, Knight considered "that a more important and more consistently motivating secret of Byron's life lay somewhere within the area of homosexuality."

The most influential of Byron's many female biographers was Doris Langley Moore, whose infatuation with Byron led her to attack anyone who discredited him. (When Ms. Langley Moore was married, the ceremony was performed over Byron's Tomb in Hucknall Church.) Although Langley Moore could not totally discount Byron's homoerotic attachments, she cut them to the bare minimum, opining that for many years of his life, "he was not interested in any male." (1974) What she failed to grasp is that when men in England could be hanged for having sex with other males, Byron necessarily concealed such relations.

In 1985 the gay historian Louis Crompton (1985) connected the dots throughout Marchand's work and concluded that Byron, both in practice and in consciousness, qualified as a gay man.

Another Marchand successor, Fiona MacCarthy, was given full access to the John Murray archives, with no constraints. MacCarthy dared to assert that Byron was more strongly attracted to males than to females. As a result, her fine biography was coldly received by the Byron establishment. In her Introduction MacCarthy makes two important points: "Our understanding of Byron's bisexuality, an open secret within his own close circle, throws important light on the pattern of his life." Yes, indeed, it is necessary to acknowledge Byron's homoeroticism in order to understand his life and his work; and yes, of course, those in Byron's circle knew that he was gay.

In a recent book, Peter Cochran (2010) quotes from a letter Shelley wrote to his good friend, Thomas Love Peacock:

> He [Byron] associates with wretches who seem almost to have lost the gait & physiognomy of man, & do not scruple to avow practices which are not only not named but I believe seldom even conceived in England. He says he disapproves, but he endures. (17 or 18 December 1818)

In other words, Byron is hanging out with screaming queans. This is a case study on how to read passages that English gay men wrote in the 19th century. Obviously, since sex between males was a hanging offence, they had to be cautious. Cochran merely comments that "Shelley may be being polite" in attributing the inconceivable practices to the malformed wretches rather than to Byron himself. Other critics have read homophobia into the passage. But Shelley is writing ironically and defensively. In another case, Cochran does grasp the principle involved: "Fearful that his letters would be opened, C.S. Matthews [Byron's gay friend at Cambridge] had to take refuge behind a facade of pretended horror." In Shelley's letter, he is writing as one of the initiated to another, feigning horror as Matthews did. The unnameable practices allude to the crime of sodomy (or buggery). "Seldom even conceived" is written in jest. Read with the proper inflection, the passage almost becomes camp.

From November 1816 to December 1819 Byron was living in Venice, where there was a large and vibrant gay community. Thanks to the *Code Napoléon*, sodomy was not punished in most of Italy, and Venice had no laws against sex between males, either civil or criminal. At the same time, sex between males was still a hanging offense in England. In addition, Venice was and still is a magically beautiful city, closely tied to Greece, which in its layout "provided unparalleled opportunities for clandestine meetings". (Wasserman)

Gay men exuberantly took part in the Venetian Carnival. The traditional Carnival costumes, the *volto* and *tabarro*, disguised the features and physiognomy so that "it was impossible to tell whether the masked wearer was male or female." (Wasserman) But as always, guys with good bodies wanted to show them off, and they wore skin-tight garments and masks to impersonate Hermes, Eros, Pan, or Harlequin. Wasserman quotes a passage from Byron's *Beppo*, which sings the delights of the Venetian Carnival:

The moment Night with dusky mantle covers
  The skies (and the more duskily the better)
The Time — less liked by husbands than by lovers —
  Begins, and Prudery flings aside her fetter,
And Gaiety on restless tiptoe hovers.
  Giggling with all the Gallants who beset her;
And there are Songs, and quavers, roaring, humming,
Guitars, and every other sort of strumming.

We note Byron's use of "Gaiety", which in context is almost certainly a code word for the initiated. This passage — like the Byron poem, "So, we'll go no more a-roving" — celebrates *cruising*, a slang word known to all sexually active gay men. "Less liked by husbands than by lovers" means *less liked by straight men than by gay men,* to whom the Carnival night belongs.

Byron was a bundle of contradictions. A wealthy peer of the Realm, his early childhood was spent in poverty. Shy, pale and effeminate, short and with a strong tendency to become fat, crippled with a foot deformity, he nevertheless became the reigning male sex symbol of the 19th century. To this day the Byronic hero is the archetype of the swaggering male adventurer, with his sardonic and defiant virility. Byron had an abundance of character defects — he could be mean and petty to even his best friends — but he also had charm and a gift for empathy, which gained lasting devotion from those close to him.

Byron had what may be called gay consciousness: he had gay friends from Cambridge, with whom he used private code words derived from Greek myth and Roman literature — for example, *hyacinths,* referring to the myth of Apollo and his love for the beautiful youth, Hyacinth. (Crompton 1985) He was conversant with underground slang or "flash language". (Dyer)

Byron was an adept at camp. Accused of carrying off a girl from a convent, he wrote, in an 1819 letter to Richard Belgrave Hoppner: "I should like to know *who* has been carried off — except poor dear *me* — I have been more ravished myself than anybody since the Trojan war." Fiona MacCarthy comments: "Here is Byron as progenitor of a high camp English manner of expression that extends to Oscar Wilde, Ronald Firbank, and Noël Coward."

Xavier Mayne, in his 1909 book *The Intersexes* regards Byron as "more or less temperamentally homosexual: an idealistic, hellenic, romantic homosexual." He asserts that "it is to be doubted if Byron really ever loved any woman....", that "Byron despised women." Mayne explicitly links Byron's Hellenism to his passion for Greek Love: "Greek in his intellectual and sexual nature, he was Englishman by birth but Athenian by heart." (Mayne)

Mayne discusses the possibility that Byron's important poem *Manfred* may represent a "homosexual allegory"; he quotes from a letter in his possession:

> When my grandfather had finished his account, which you can imagine was done with great embarrassment, Byron said after a moment — "Pooh. I don't think any the worse of you for such an affair.... Why, let me tell you I expected awhile ago to write a drama on Greek Love — not less — modernizing the atmosphere — glooming it over — to throw the whole subject back into nature, where it belongs now as always — to paint the struggle of the finer moral type of mind against it — or rather remorse for it, when it seems to be chastised.... But I made up my mind that British philosophy is not far enough on for swallowing such a think neat. So I turned much of it into 'Manfred'."

And Mayne concludes:

> We may then argue "Manfred" as, in a sense, an uranian drama, according to the foregoing: a sexual love between Manfred and a youth, or some more mature friend, as the burden on the conscience of Manfred — or rather the loss that oppresses him. Astarte thus becomes a psychic allegory: under her feminine personality is hidden a male relationship.

Mayne's insight, that Byron has hidden a male relationship under a female persona, is supported by the examples of Shelley ("Kissing Helena", "To Stella", the lady in "Julian and Maddalo", Emily in "Epipsychidion") and also by Byron's own poem, "Thyrza" (which ought to have been, "Edlestone"). For the sake of alliteration it is tempting to say that Manfred is a cousin to Shelley's "Maniac" (*Julian and Maddalo*) and "Monster" (*Frankenstein*) — all being disguised personifications of homoerotic desire in a context of shame and horror.

After the 1985 publication of *Byron and Greek Love* by gay scholar Louis Crompton, even the typical professor of English literature was obliged to acknowledge that Byron's sexual preference was for teenaged boys ... that Byron had gay friends from Cambridge, with whom he corresponded using private code words ("hyacinths", etc.) ... that "Thyrza" is a nonce feminine name entitling a poem that is really about Edlestone, a choirboy with whom Byron was deeply in love.

We now know with certainty that Byron and his friends proudly accepted their sexuality, at least in private. What are the biographical implications? Let's begin with the friendship between Byron and Shelley, which lasted from 1816, when they met, until 1822, when Shelley died. This is one of the great literary friendships, one that transformed the lives and work of both men. John Addington Symonds observes that Byron, the senior poet, pursued Shelley, changing his own residence in order to be near him. (Symonds) Well now, in the six years that they knew each other, during the many hundreds of hours they spent in conversation together, did they ever discuss male love? Of course they did, although one would hardly know it from their pusillanimous biographers. And it follows that they also discussed male love with their close friends, the men in the Shelley-Byron circle. I am not suggesting that the relationship between Byron and Shelley was sexual. My guess is that they were not each other's type.

Byron strongly preferred all-male society. According to a major biographer, from 1816 in Switzerland: "the evenings at Diodati were masculine ones. Shelley came alone, but Byron pacified the ladies by calling occasionally at Shelley's cottage." (Marchand) By 1821, when Byron and the Shelley circle were living in Pisa, there were no longer even token visits to Shelley's residence. (Byron despised Mary Shelley, although he was courteous and provided employment for her after Shelley's death.) Instead, Shelley, Medwin, Williams, and later Trelawny visited Byron's palazzo, the Casa Lanfranchi, on an almost daily basis for pistol shooting, billiards, and conversation. In December Byron began giving weekly stag parties for his small circle of friends, with fine food and wine; often he and his guests "talked over their wine until two or three in the morning." The ladies were never invited. (Marchand, Lovell 1966) Male love was surely one of the topics they talked about during these gatherings.

Byron's biographers have strained mightily to heterosexualize his life, for example, by overemphasizing his boyhood crush on Mary Chaworth, a girl several years older than he. The time has come to re-evaluate this and other relationships, such as his famous affair with Countess Teresa Guiccioli.

The very young Countess Teresa, or "La Guiccioli" as Byron and his friends affectionately called her, left her husband — the "evil" Count Guiccioli, a man forty years older than she — for Byron. Alhough their affair is always assumed to be sexual, it may not have been. In her old age Teresa insisted that it had been only platonic. Commenting on Byron's biographers she declared:

> In all their writings they have romanticized my person, and converted into love and passion a sentiment which no one has the right to see in any other light than that of a warm and enthusiastic friendship. (Origo)

Her biographer Iris Origo comments: "Self-delusion, surely, can go no further." But perhaps Teresa was telling the truth. There are subtle indications in her reminiscences of Byron, written in old age, that she knew he loved other males and accepted this. (Guiccioli) Perhaps she was one of those women, now known as "fag hags", who are attracted to gay men. It may be significant that Teresa was fond of Byron's friends, and they were fond of her. Teresa neither lived in Byron's palazzo in Pisa nor entered it. When he wished to see her, he went to her residence. (Marchand)

In 1826, two years after Byron's death, Teresa returned to her husband, the evil Count, then separated from him a second time. Eventually he died. Teresa travelled to England several times; made friends; and had affairs with attractive, sensitive young men. At the age of forty-seven she married the Marquis de Boissy, "an eccentric, generous and witty middle-aged peer, and one of the richest men in France", and they lived happily until his death in 1866. Even in old age she was regarded as charming and affectionate. (Origo)

Biographers tend to neglect Teresa's handsome younger brother, Count Pietro Gamba, who was Byron's constant companion for the last four years of his life. On 29 July 1820, Byron wrote Teresa: "I like your little brother very much...." Within two months Pietro had become "Pierino" to Byron, and closer to him than Teresa. (Origo) When Byron departed for Greece in 1823, to fight for Greek independence, he took Pietro with him, but left Teresa behind. A grief-stricken Pietro was at Byron's bedside when he died in 1824. Pietro accompanied Byron's remains back to England, where he wrote an account of the poet's last year. Then he returned to Greece, where he died in 1827, only about twenty-four years of age. (Marchand, Gamba, Origo)

We shall never know the full extent to which the works of Byron and Shelley have been suppressed or bowdlerized. According to Byron scholar the late Peter Cochran, two stanzas of *Childe Harold's Pilgrimage* (*CHP*), alluding to Byron's homoerotic adventures in 1811, were suppressed by R.C. Dallas, "who introduced Byron to the market-conscious John Murray." In consequence, "thanks to legions of pure, fastidious editors, the poem's confessional message has been muted out of existence ever since." (Cochran) In his Internet edition of *CHP* Cochran has restored the expurgated stanzas. Here is one, describing the court of Ali Pasha in Albania:

> Here woman's voice is never heard — apart,
> And scarce permitted guarded, veiled to rove,
> She yields to one her person & her heart,
> Tamed to her cage, nor feels a wish to move,
> For boyish minions of unhallowed love
> The shameless torch of wild desire is lit,
> Caressed, preferred even woman's self above,
> Whose forms for Nature's gentler errors fit
> All frailties mote excuse save that which they commit.

Don Juan (*DJ*), considered Byron's masterpiece, is a very long poem — thousands of stanzas, each with over sixty words. I suspect that few have ever read all of it. At times *DJ* can be tiresome, but at its best *DJ* is brilliant satire on a wide range of themes, including politics, literature, religion, and sex. *DJ* is permeated with *camp*, and is best read by gay men, who know the conventions, rhythms, and language of camp. (For brief examples, the empress of Russia, Catherine the Great, is described as "This modern Amazon and queen of queans"; her attraction to Juan is explained: "Besides, the empress sometimes liked a boy."

The women in *DJ* all have powerful sexual urges, which are directed towards the eponymous hero, Don Juan, who in the course of the poem passes from late adolescence to early manhood (late teens to early twenties, which the late Warren Johansson called the "classic age of the hustler"). "Juan, with his virgin face" is pursued, but does not pursue; he is "always the seduced, but not the seducer ... the passive victim of active women." (Cochran) The male narrator of *DJ* is clearly in love with Juan — who is in love with himself: "He, on the other hand, if not in love, / Fell into that no less imperious passion, / Self-love...." (*DJ*, Canto IX: LXVIII).

Byron delights in dressing up Juan, just as in real life he enjoyed dressing up his boys — he called them "pages" — from Robert Rushton in 1808 to Lukas Chalandritsanos in 1824. In Russia, Juan is dressed up in uniform to please the lusty and super-dominant Catherine the Great. In a long comic episode Juan is kidnapped and held in a seraglio, where he is forced to wear women's clothes. The poor boy didn't really want to, but once dressed up, he makes the best of it. When the Sultan inspects his seraglio, his eye immediately picks out Juan from the hundreds of concubines:

His Highness cast around his great black eyes,
    And looking, as he always looked, perceived
Juan amongst his damsels in disguise;
    At which he seemed no whit surprized nor grieved,
But just remarked, with air sedate and wise,
    While still a fluttering sigh Gulbeyaz heaved,
"I see you've bought another Girl, 'tis pity
That a mere Christian should be half so pretty."
        (*DJ* CLV)

DJ is filled with *double entendres* and in-group references hinting at male love. In four lines Byron pointedly discloses that he is writing for the *initiated* — a word that the Shelley-Byron men used as a code word for *gay*.

The grand Arcanum's not for men to see all;
    My Music hath some mystic diapasons,
And there is much which could not be appreciated
In any manner by the uninitiated.
    (*DJ* XIV, 22, 5-8)

One of Byron's most obvious hints to the initiated is in the couplet:

> But Virgil's songs are pure, except that horrid one
> Beginning with 'Formosum Pastor Corydon'
> (*DJ*, Canto I: XLII).

Byron is camping here, and "horrid" is mock disapproval. The reference is to Virgil's Second Eclogue, where the shepherd Corydon expresses his burning love for the boy Alexis, his master's darling. This is significant, because for centuries the Eclogue has been used by gay men to identify each other — along with such references as Shakespeare's sonnets, Antinoüs, Orestes and Pylades, Achilles and Patroklos, David and Jonathan, and so on. Byron is saying to the initiated that he is one of us.

Although women went wild over Byron's earlier poems, many of them (including his mistress, Countess Teresa Guiccioli) were hostile to *DJ*, which not only had pederastic overtones, but made fun of women's hypocrisy, sentimentality, and self-delusion.

Since the last four cantos of *Don Juan* were destroyed after Byron's death, we have no idea how he would have concluded it.

Byron biographers, even including openly gay Louis Crompton, have given the impression that Byron was not attracted to post-adolescent males. While it is true that we lack forensic evidence of Byron's sex acts with other adult males, we should not expect to find such evidence, considering that Byron's very survival depended on discretion, that his writings were expurgated during his lifetime, and his letters and *Memoir* were burned after his death.

But, in fact, there is some evidence that Byron was attracted to post-adolescent males. Take William Fletcher, who "was at Byron's side from 1804, when Byron was sixteen, almost without interval until his master died." (MacCarthy) The teenaged Byron had spied the teenaged Fletcher plowing the fields and then taken him on as his valet or personal servant. Well now, the Fletcher behind the plow may have had a good body, but did this qualify him to be a valet ("gentlemen's gentleman"), whose duties included taking care of clothes and other personal services?

In 1809 Byron and Fletcher were travelling in Portugal, where they visited a monastery: "Fletcher complained that the 'benevolent faced clergyman' had been teaching him Greek and kissing him." (MacCarthy) So, Fletcher in his early twenties was good-looking, and didn't resist being kissed by a clergyman. In 1814 Byron and Fletcher, then in their mid-twenties, were living in a Piccadilly apartment where, after exercise, Byron would "get Fletcher to rub him down." (MacCarthy) When a gay man receives a massage from a handsome and well built young man — a young man he is paying to perform personal services — we may imagine that the massages become erotic and one thing leads to another. Why not?

When Fletcher was in his early thirties he was still good-looking and had flaxen hair, according to an 1821 letter written by Percy Bysshe Shelley. At Byron's funeral, overcome with grief, Fletcher collapsed and had to support himself against a pew. This is more like the reaction of a lover than just a loyal servant.

Another servant was Giovanni Battista Falcieri, known as "Tita", a muscular young gondolier he had acquired in Venice. The gondoliers of Venice were renowned for selling their sexual services. Apparently Tita had sex (for "broad silver pieces") with a Byron guest, William Bankes, who had initiated Byron into the gay world at Cambridge. (MacCarthy)

Whether or not he had sex with them, Byron liked the company of handsome young men. These would include his travelling companion, Dr. John Polidori; his companion for the last four years of his life, Count Pietro ("Pierino") Gamba; as well as Edward John Trelawny, Percy Bysshe Shelley, and Edward Ellerker Williams. In London Byron frequented a boxing club, which was patronized by wealthy men. Very likely the boxers did a bit of hustling on the side.

After Byron's death, his memoirs were burned by his publisher and literary executor. Testimony concerning the memoirs, from those who claimed to have read them, is so extremely contradictory that we can only speculate as to their contents. In my opinion it is likely that they dealt with male love, and included a plea for its emancipation.

Now, let's turn to the lesser figures in the Shelley-Byron Circle.

III. Thomas Medwin

Thomas Medwin was born in 1788 into a wealthy and well connected family in Horsham, Sussex. He and Shelley were second cousins, who had known each other well from earliest childhood. Their homes were only two miles apart. Medwin was already at Syon House Academy when Shelley entered it at the age of ten. There he was able to provide some solace for his younger cousin, who was the target of bullying. Medwin records an early episode of Shelley's life-long habit of sleep walking:

> He was subject to strange, and sometimes frightful dreams, and was haunted by apparitions that bore all the semblance of reality. We did not sleep in the same dormitory, but I shall never forget one moonlight night seeing Shelley walk into my room. He was in a state of somnambulism. His eyes were open, and he advanced with slow steps to the window, which, it being the height of summer, was open. (Medwin 1847/1913)

After a year in a public school Medwin matriculated at Oxford in 1805, and he left a few years later without taking his degree. After living in London for awhile, he sailed for India in 1812, becoming Lieutenant in His Majesty's 24th Light Dragoons, where he remained for about seven years. Apart from his military duties he hunted, fished, travelled throughout India, pursued independent study, and became an excellent writer. When his regiment disbanded in 1819, he retired on half pay and moved to Geneva, along with his younger friend, Edward Ellerker Williams, also a half-pay lieutenant, and Williams's common-law wife, Jane. (Lovell 1962)

In 1820 Medwin finished his first published poem, *Oswald and Edwin, An Oriental Sketch,* which he dedicated to Williams, "as a slight memorial of a long and uninterrupted intimacy, commenced amid the scenes it attempts to revive, ... by His Affectionate Friend, T. Medwin." (Medwin 1820/1978) The 42-page poem is about romantic friendship between two young men, one of whom is killed. In the same year the first child was born to Edward and Jane; they named him Edward Medwin Williams, and for some years they called him Medwin. Many years later Medwin wrote of this period in his life:

> Williams and myself had hunted the tiger in another hemisphere, and had been constant correspondents

> in India, and on my return home took a *compagne* together at Geneva, and revived a friendship such as I have never felt for any other individual. A more noble, unworldly being never existed than Williams. (Medwin 1847/1913)

In the fall of 1820 Medwin joined Shelley in Pisa. For four months the two cousins, reunited after an absence of seven years, collaborated intensely in translating Greek and German.

Unfortunately, Shelley's second wife Mary became jealous — the two men would go off to study together or would discuss things that were over her head — so she eventually drove Medwin away, stating in a letter to her stepsister, Claire Clairmont, that she and Shelley found him a "seccatura" (should have been *seccatore*: bore, nuisance) and "Common Place personified". In truth, Shelley never found Medwin boring or "common place", nor ever said an unkind word about him. Shelley later apologized to Medwin for Mary's rudeness and urged him to return to Pisa, which he did later in 1821.

After a period of travel — to Rome, Venice, and Geneva — Medwin returned to Pisa to meet Byron, who arrived with his entourage in late 1821. They were compatible. Often after one of Byron's stag dinners, Medwin and he would remain, talking over their wine after the other guests had left, into the wee hours of the morning. On these occasions, Medwin took notes.

After the deaths of Shelley (July 1822) and Byron (April 1824) Medwin's life became a bit of a mess. He married a Swedish heiress, squandered her entire fortune in four years, and then abandoned her and their two daughters. His father disinherited him. The rest of his life, although highly productive from a literary standpoint, was spent in near poverty. He died in 1869, aged 81. On his tombstone is engraved: "He was a friend and companion of Byron, Shelley, and Trelawny."

For our purposes Medwin is important as the first biographer of both Byron and Shelley. His *Journal of the Conversations of Lord Byron: Noted during a Residence with His Lordship at Pisa, in the Years 1821 and 1822* was published in 1824. It was a scandal and an immediate success, which eventually went through fifteen different editions and translations. In the words of Medwin's biographer:

> ... after the appearance of the *Conversations* one of the greatest storms in English literary history broke, and the view of him is thereafter often clouded — by hatred, hurt, and fear of damaged reputations. For Medwin was to become midwife to a dead man, whose voice came back from the grave to laugh and sneer at the living. (Lovell 1962)

A smear campaign against Medwin was launched. He became, in Lovell's words, "one of the most outrageously misrepresented men in all literary history."

Every mistake he made, and there were many, was imputed to incompetence or dishonesty. Later biographers felt obliged to write with disdain of the man whose writings they freely plundered for material. By 1989 a Mary Shelley biographer (Sunstein), following the pack, felt she could refer to Medwin as "stupid".

Stupid, Medwin was not. He was a good classical scholar who, partly in collaboration with Shelley, translated the complete tragedies of Aeschylus. His travel writings are first rate. In addition to Greek, Medwin read and translated Latin, Spanish, Italian, Portuguese, French, and German. Dozens of his works were published during his lifetime. Both Byron and Shelley accepted him as an intellectual peer as well as a friend.

For the discerning reader, the *Conversations* contain many subtle clues and hints as to Byron's sexual preferences. (Lovell 1966 for the following) Medwin gives a very flattering description of Countess Teresa Guiccioli and then comments: "Lord Byron is certainly very much attached to her, without being actually in love."

Medwin reports Byron as recalling with distaste his affair with the nymphomaniacal Lady Caroline Lamb:

> The lady had scarcely any personal attractions to recommend her. Her figure, though genteel, was too thin to be good, and wanted that roundness which elegance and grace would vainly supply.

In Medwin's account, Byron recalls an occasion when she gained entrance to his apartment when he was away and, finding a book on the table, wrote on the first page, "Remember me!" When Byron found it, he wrote two stanzas under it, the final one being:

> Remember thee! Ay, doubt it not;
> Thy husband too shall think of thee;
> By neither shalt thou be forgot,
> Thou *false* to him, thou *fiend* to me!

We learn from Medwin that Byron in his youth had mingled with the London dandies and was proud of his friendship with Beau Brummell. Byron was also a friend of Matthew G. ("Monk") Lewis, who visited him in Italy. Medwin quotes Byron as saying:

> Lewis was a pleasant companion, and would always have remained a boy in spirits and manners — (unlike me!). He was fond of the society of younger men than himself. I myself never knew a man, except Shelley, who was companionable till thirty. I remember Mrs. Hope once asking who was Lewis's male-love this season.

Medwin was the first to write on the life of his cousin Shelley, and he was one of the first to champion him as a great poet. Many of Shelley's poems were rescued from oblivion by Medwin. His first writings on Shelley were published in *The Athenaeum*, beginning in 1832. Over the opposition of Mary Shelley, he wrote a two-volume biography of Shelley, which was published in 1847; a revised and expanded version of this was published long after Medwin's death, edited with intense hostility by H. Buxton Forman. (The following based on Medwin 1847/1913)

In his *Life of Percy Bysshe Shelley* Medwin provides subtle clues as to Shelley's sexual preferences. He prints for the first time Shelley's descriptions of two sculptures in the Uffizi gallery in Florence, "Laocoön" and "Bacchus and Ampelus" — written with great enthusiasm for the beauty of the adolescent male. An excerpt from "Bacchus and Ampelus":

> Ampelus, with a young lion's or lynx's skin over his shoulders, holds a cup in his right hand and with his left half encircles Bacchus, as you may have seen a younger and an elder boy at school, walking in some grassy spot of the playground, with that tender friendship for each other that the age inspires. The countenance of Bacchus is sublimely sweet and lovely, taking a shade of gentle and playful tenderness from the arch looks of Ampelus, whose cheerful face turned towards him, expresses the suggestion of some droll and merry device.

Medwin pointedly observes that Mary Shelley left these out of *Shelley's Posthumous Works* ("But there are two groups which Mrs. Shelley has omitted in her Work of Love, and which I shall give in his own words...."). This amounts to a rebuke, and indicates that he wished, within the limits of discretion, to counteract the Shelley Legend which Mary had begun to construct. This required some nerve on Medwin's part, as she had established a proprietary claim on Shelley — a man she understood and appreciated far less than did his male friends — a man who, for the last year of his life, avoided even eating breakfast with her.

Throughout the book are scattered hints of homoeroticism — for example, an oblique reference to a bisexual Italian who "had a predilection for our *compatriotes* with and without the e...." Medwin comments that the young Count Gamba (Byron's "Pierino") "carried with him the passport of a very handsome person". He establishes the relationship between Shelley and Edward Williams as one of love and that between Shelley and Jane Williams as purely one of friendship. Medwin supplies the text of Shelley's "Epitaph for Two Friends", and states that it was written for Williams. He also indicates that Shelley and Williams are the two characters in "Boat on the Serchio". (More about these two poems below in the section under Williams.)

IV. Edward John Trelawny

Edward John Trelawny was born into an old, upper-class Cornish family. A rebellious boy, he was sent by his father to a boarding school that resembled a reformatory. When that failed to curb his rebelliousness, he was sent into the Navy at the age of twelve or thirteen. After six years at sea, he returned to England, married, had two children, divorced, and then travelled to Geneva, where he met Medwin and Williams.

In January of 1822, he arrived in Pisa. Twenty-nine at the time, the same age as Shelley, Trelawny was tall, dark, and handsome. His appearance was exotic; his physique was impressive. Byron and Shelley immediately accepted him as a friend.

Trelawny's *Recollections of the Last Days of Shelley and Byron,* published thirty-six years later, is a superb literary biography, a precious document of English Romanticism. Although he only knew Shelley for the last half year of his life, Trelawny fell immediately in love, a love which lasted for the rest of his long life. His description of their first meeting is unforgettable:

> Swiftly gliding in, blushing like a girl, a tall thin stripling held out both his hands; and although I could hardly believe as I looked at his flushed, feminine, and artless face that it could be the Poet, I returned his warm pressure. (Trelawny 1858)

Trelawny's bravado enables him to get away with outrageous or indiscreet statements. For example, he gives a long, loving description of Shelley's appearance and body and casually remarks that he loved Shelley, that he and Shelley loved Williams, and that Williams and Hogg loved Shelley. (Trelawny 1858, Massingham, Smith)

The *Recollections* are filled with ambiguous hints of homoeroticism — for example, in describing Shelley's boat, the Don Juan:

> She was fast, strongly built, and Torbay rigged. I despatched her under charge of two steady seamen, and a smart sailor lad, named Charles Vivian. Shelley sent back the two sailors and only retained the boy.... (Trelawny 1858)

Here one notices the phrase, "smart sailor lad", which seems to imply that the boy was attractive. Is there a further implication that he was retained because of his looks? When the boat went down in a storm two months later, Charles Vivian died along with Shelley and Williams.

Like Medwin, Trelawny has been treated viciously by biographers — portrayed as a nonentity, who imposed himself on the Pisan circle, and as an inveterate liar. The former is untrue and unfair: if Shelley and Byron welcomed the friendship of Trelawny, it was because, to their credit, they recognized and responded to his imagination and talent. So far as Trelawny's veracity is concerned, most of the charges here stem from a misreading of his first book, *Adventures of a Younger Son.*

Younger Son, published anonymously in 1831, is a thrilling adventure story and contains some of the finest English prose of the 19th century. Although Trelawny privately described it as his autobiography, he cannot have meant this literally. It should be obvious to anyone who can read, that *Younger Son* is a work of fiction — an autobiographical novel, yes, but above all a product of imagination. It is absurd to imagine that the narrator's adventures as a teenaged pirate, his child bride Zela, killed by sharks, and so on, literally represented the *facts* of Trelawny's life. On the other hand, Trelawny did say, and repeatedly, that his life was in the book. The question therefore arises: What in the book is true?

I submit that one true thing in the book is Trelawny's experience of male love, which he describes with passion and candor. (See Appendix III: Edward John Trelawny.) Trelawny always insisted that a character in the novel, De Ruyter, was a real man, and I believe him. De Ruyter may not have been his name, and he was probably not a pirate, but there must have been a man of about thirty who was lover and mentor to a teenaged Trelawny.

In later life Trelawny refused to go along with the Saintly Shelley legend. He expressed outrage when Mary Shelley published a bowdlerized version of *Queen Mab* with the anti-religious notes omitted. In his last published work Trelawny affirmed that Shelley, "from the earliest stage of his career to the last day of his life ... ignored all religions as superstitions." Trelawny's last words on Shelley are:

> A clergyman wrote in the visitors' book at the Mer de Glace, Chamouni, something to the following effect: 'No one can view this sublime scene, and deny the existence of God.' Under which Shelley, using a Greek phrase, wrote, 'P.B. Shelley, Atheist,' thereby proclaiming his opinion to all the world. And he never regretted having done this. (Trelawny 1878)

Trelawny had wives, children, and mistresses. He took up farming. In old age he lived alone with his dogs, alternating between a house in London and one on the south coast. He adhered to a vegetarian diet, abstained from alcohol, took a cold bath every day, walked a lot, and swam in all seasons. A man who observed him stripping for a swim said that Trelawny, then in his eighties, still had a fine, muscular physique.

When Trelawny finally died, at the age of 89, his ashes were buried next to Shelley's in the Protestant

Cemetery in Rome, in a grave he had reserved almost 60 years earlier.

V. Edward Ellerker Williams

Edward Ellerker Williams was born in 1793, into an upper-middle class family. In 1805 he was at Eton, but didn't know Shelley there. He entered the British Navy at eleven years of age, then left the Navy and went into the Army, and was sent to India. He retired from the Eighth Dragoons in 1816 and moved to Geneva with his common-law wife, Jane.

In 1821 Thomas Medwin introduced Edward and Jane Williams to Shelley, in the hope that they "would form the charm of his solitary life", which they did. In 1822 Williams and Shelley died in a boating accident, both aged twenty nine.

If Williams is remembered now, it is as the "inseparable companion" of Shelley for the last year of their lives. He must have been an amiable young man: Medwin, Trelawny, Shelley, and Jane Williams all loved him; Byron received frequent visits from him; and even Mary Shelley, so often critical of males in the Shelley-Byron circle, was fond of him.

It is my thesis that Williams and Shelley were lovers, at least in the sense that they loved each other and were regarded as a couple by their close male friends. Intuitively I believe that they had sex together, but there is little chance of proving this now, almost two centuries after their deaths.

The testimonies of Thomas Medwin, Edward John Trelawny, and even Mary Shelley agree that, from the time they met each other, Shelley and Williams were close, "inseparable" companions. Shelley's health and appearance improved dramatically, and the final year of his life was his happiest. Trelawny says directly that Shelley loved Williams and that Williams loved Shelley; there is no reason to assume he was using hyperbole.

When reading Shelley's poetry many years ago, I did a double-take on the following poem, immediately recognizing its homoerotic implications of two friends being buried together.

EPITAPH

These are two friends whose lives were undivided;
So let their memory be, now they have glided
Under the grave; let not their bones be parted
For their two hearts in life were single-hearted.
(Shelley/Hutchinson 1970)

Then I learned from Medwin's *Life* that Shelley had himself and Williams in mind when he wrote the epitaph, of which Medwin gives the following version:

EPITAPH

They were two friends, whose life was undivided.
So let them mingle. Sweetly they had glided
Under the grave. Let not their dust be parted,
For their two hearts in life were single-hearted.
(Medwin 1847/1913)

However, neither version follows Shelley's manuscript. H. Buxton Forman provides the following note:

> This version of the epitaph may perchance have been written by Shelley: probably more than one manuscript exists. The best version is that of the holograph in Mr. Bixley's Note Book No. I:
>
> These are two friends whose lives were undivided —
> So let their memory be now they have glided
> Under the grave, let not their bones be parted
> For their two breasts in life were single-hearted.
>
> The Medwin variant might be recorded in variorum editions of Shelley with a caution. Mary Shelley had the Note Book in question when she first published the epitaph in 1824; and, if that was her sole source, she must have misread *breasts* for *hearts*, which scarcely makes sense, although it has satisfied editors and critics so far. Although written in pencil, the words are all absolutely unmistakable. (Medwin 1913)

As Forman points out, the final line makes no sense when "two hearts" is substituted for "two breasts". However, Mary Shelley may not simply have "misread breasts for hearts", but deliberately altered the line to obscure its physicality. Two breasts is potentially erotic; two hearts is not. Mary did her best to censor homoeroticism in Shelley's works — for example, her unforgivable suppression and then bowdlerization of Shelley's translation of Plato's dialogue on Eros, *The Banquet* (or *Symposium*), which was only published complete and unbowdlerized more than a century after Shelley finished it.

At any rate, the epitaph is undeniably an expression of love. According to Medwin, Shelley showed all of his poems to Williams, including those written to Jane Williams, and so we may imagine them discussing variants of the epitaph. As it turned out, they had only a few months to live. It is my belief that after Trelawny and Byron cremated Shelley and Williams, they mixed their ashes together to honor their desire to be buried together. (For a fuller account: http://paganpressbooks.com/jpl/ASHES.HTM .)

The relationship between Shelley and Williams is charmingly depicted in "The Boat on the Serchio". In introducing this poem Medwin comments, "I have heard Shelley often speak with rapture of the excursions they made together." (Medwin 1847/1913) Melchior and Lionel represent Shelley and Williams. The playful banter of the two friends, as they prepare for a boating excursion, could almost be that of a present-day male couple sailing in Provincetown in the summer. It may be the happiest poem Shelley ever wrote.

Lionel and Melchior are obviously fond of and at ease with each other. One line hints that they share a common bed, and in the final stanza Shelley communicates to the "discerning few" that their relationship is sexual. The "death which lovers love" can only mean *orgasm*, which rhymes with the terminal words in lines 3, 5, and 7. This may be the grandest portrayal of orgasm in all of literature:

also discussed in Gay and Lesbian Review, Sept-Oct 2002, p. 12

The Serchio, twisting forth
Between the marble barriers which it clove
At Ripafratta, leads through the dread chasm
The wave that died the death which lovers love,
Living in what it sought; as if this spasm
Had not yet passed, the toppling mountains cling,
But the clear stream in full enthusiasm
Pours itself on the plain, then wandering
Down one clear path of effluence crystalline
Sends its superfluous waves, that they may fling
At Arno's feet tribute of corn and wine;
Then, through the pestilential deserts wild
Of tangled marsh and woods of stunted pine,
It rushes to the Ocean.

In 1822 Shelley addressed several poems to Jane Williams. Solely on this basis, biographers have leapt to the conclusion that Shelley loved Jane Williams or even that they were having an affair. The poems are lovely and charming, especially "With A Guitar" and "The Keen Stars Were Twinkling", but there is nothing in them to suggest that his affection for her amounted to anything approaching romantic love. Shelley was indeed fond of Jane, but it was as a dear friend and as the wife of Edward.

In "With A Guitar", Shelley adopts characters from The Tempest, casting himself as Ariel (the airy spirit), Jane as Miranda, and Edward as Prince Ferdinand. The following lines are significant:

> For by permission and command
> Of thine own Prince Ferdinand,
> Poor Ariel sends this silent token
> Of more than ever can be spoken....

In other words, Shelley is writing a poem to Jane with the knowledge, and at the express wish, of Edward. If the poem expresses fondness for Jane, one might also say that writing it was a way of expressing love for Edward — like presenting flowers to the wife of one's best friend when dining at her house.

Medwin emphatically denies there was anything improper in the relationship between Shelley and Jane:

> The verses addressed to her always passed through the hands of Williams himself, who had too much confidence in the virtue of one devotedly his, to harbour for a moment any jealousy of an attachment the most innocent and disinterested. Effusions such as these must not be interpreted literally. (Medwin 1847/1913)

The way that biographers have treated Shelley's relationship to Edward and Jane Williams provides an example of the evidentiary double standard that prevails in the realm of sexuality. On the one hand, evidence suggesting homoerotic desire or activity must be practically sufficient for a criminal conviction. On the other hand, where heterosexual activity or desire is concerned, any rumor, any fantasy, any reference in a poem will do, even if contradicted by evidence. Medwin, Trelawny, and Shelley all bear testimony to love between Shelley and Edward. At the same time, there is no evidence whatever that Shelley and Jane were in love with each other, let alone were having an affair.

VI. Thomas Jefferson Hogg

Thomas Jefferson Hogg was born into a wealthy professional family in 1792. He matriculated at Oxford in 1810, where he soon became Shelley's bosom friend. Though their personalities were complementary, they shared a contempt for superstition and conventional opinion. The two were expelled from Oxford together, when they were both eighteen, over a pamphlet they had published, "The Necessity of Atheism". They then lived together in London until they were separated by their families. As described above, Shelley's letters to Hogg are those of a man to his lover.

Hogg's reminiscences of Shelley, written thirty-six years after his death, are a loving tribute and include numerous hints as to male love. (For an example see Appendix IV.) Hogg includes Shelley's "Essay on Friendship", which describes his love for another schoolboy. Dedicated to Hogg, it was written in the last year of his life.

Critics have charged that Hogg, in his *Life of Percy Bysshe Shelley*, condescended to, or ridiculed, or even betrayed his friend. On the contrary, Hogg fondly remembers a romantic male friendship — two brilliant young men who were heretical, sometimes reckless, sometimes silly, and very much attached to each other.

One of their pranks was to publish poems, which they had intentionally made ridiculous, to "ridicule the strange mixture of sentimentality with the murderous fury of revolutionists, that was so prevalent in the compositions of the day." The handsomely produced book, entitled *Posthumous Fragments of Margaret Nicholson: Being Poems found Amongst the Papers of that Noted Female Who Attempted the Life of the King in 1786,* was published under the pseudonym of John Fitzvictor. The real Peg Nicholson, a washerwoman who had attempted to assassinate King George III with a carving knife, was still alive and residing in a lunatic asylum; but Shelley and Hogg saw "no harm in putting her to death, and in creating a nephew and administrator to the editor of his aunt's poetical works." Hogg states, tongue-in-cheek:

> I have one copy, if not more, somewhere or other, but not at hand. There were some verses, I remember, with a good deal about sucking in them; to these I objected, as unsuitable to the gravity of a university, but Shelley declared they would be the most impressive of all. (Hogg p. 161)

Presumably this refers to the following stanza, from "FRAGMENT: Supposed to be an Epithalamium of Francis Ravaillac and Charlotte Cordé":

> "SOFT, my dearest angel stay,
> "Oh! you suck my soul away;
> "Suck on, suck on, I glow, I glow!
> "Tides of maddening passion roll,
> "And streams of rapture drown my soul.
> "Now give me one more billing kiss,
> "Let your lips now repeat the bliss,
> "Endless kisses steal my breath,
> "No life can equal such a death."

Death in line 90 is a metaphor for orgasm, and the rhythmic urgency of line 84 clearly conveys the act of *fellatio*. Though ostensibly heterosexual, the stanza suggests that the two Oxford undergraduates were not unfamiliar with cocksucking.

At the end of his *Life*, Hogg reaches the point where Shelley has met Mary Wollstonecraft Godwin, the girl who would steal him away from his pregnant wife and child. Hogg poses the question, "Did he love her [Mary]?", and then poses it again, "Did he love her?" Hogg has led the reader to expect that the question will be answered, but instead he tells two stories — of teen-aged boys who loved and were loved by Shelley. The first boy, a young officer in a marching regiment, was sixteen and Shelley was twenty two when they met. The second was a close friend of Shelley, and later Hogg, from the time he left the Navy at the age of 15. The book abruptly ends, without really answering the question. This would seem to be Hogg's way of saying, slyly and indirectly, that Shelley did not ever love Mary, because his true loves were young men.

When the first two volumes of Hogg's *Life* were published in 1858, Sir Percy and Jane, Lady Shelley were not pleased; they withdrew their support and demanded the return of all materials they had lent Hogg. But first, concealing her displeasure, Lady Shelley inveigled Hogg into lending her the manuscripts of the second two volumes, which he had already completed. (Seymour) These disappeared and were never published. Most likely she destroyed them, as she did many other letters and manuscripts that did not suit the legend she was fabricating. This is a shame, as the *Life* is brilliant literature in its own right. It is also a shame that, owing to the calumnies of Lady Shelley and her followers, this work is no longer read or appreciated, except in the snippets appropriated by biographers.

The relationship between the two men had its strains, but it always survived. After Shelley left England for the final time in 1818, he never saw Hogg again, although he corresponded with him and often invited him to visit Italy.

In September 1822, following the deaths of Williams and Shelley, Jane Williams returned to London with a letter of introduction to Hogg, who was by then a successful barrister. He was soon enamored of her; and by early 1827 they were living together as a married couple, even though Jane was still legally married to her first husband. Although Hogg was disinherited by his family for this, their union was a happy one; they had one daughter, Prudentia, and Hogg was a good step-father to her children by Edward Williams. One Shelley biographer snidely comments: "True to his form of old, Hogg was soon attracted by Shelley's latest love-object." (Holmes) This is not only ungenerous, but it is based on a false premise. More believable is that Jane was an attractive, charming, and amiable woman, who genuinely loved and understood gay men. As it was, she was lucky Hogg took an interest in her, since her marital prospects were not good — she was a woman with children, without money, no longer young, the widow of a common-law husband, and with a real husband still living. Who is this ?

VII. Thomas Love Peacock

Thomas Love Peacock was born in 1785. During Shelley's lifetime, Peacock was a good friend and mentor, especially in Greek literature. After Shelley's death, Peacock was the executor of his will. Peacock was a close friend of major literary figures, including Leigh Hunt, John Stuart Mill, and Jeremy Bentham. It is interesting that his friends included both the first man (Bentham) and the second (Shelley) to write in English about sex between males.

In his "Memoirs of Percy Bysshe Shelley", written between 1858 and 1862, Peacock explains why he has previously refused to write about Shelley's life:

> If there be in the life of the subject of the biographer any event which he himself would willingly have blotted from the tablet of his own memory ... if such an event be the cardinal point of a life ... then, as there is no moral compulsion to speak of the matter

at all, it is better to let the whole story slumber in silence. (Peacock)

Shelley's sexual attraction to other males may well be what Peacock had in mind. He and Shelley shared an interest in male love. The first attested uses of the phrase "Uranian Love" in an erotic context are in 1818: Peacock used it in his long poem, "Rhododaphne"; Shelley used it in his review of "Rhododaphne", in his translation of Plato's dialogue, *The Banquet*, and in *Adonais*. (*Oxford English Dictionary*.) Peacock used it again in his dialogue novel, *Crochet Castle* (Appendix I)

Peacock is an excellent poet in his own right, and he is one of the best satirists in the English language. The passage on Uranian Love from *Crochet Castle* (Appendix I) is not only a marvelous example of high camp, but a vigorous assault on sexual hypocrisy. Later in the 19th century "Uranian" became a favored word of gay men in England. (d'Arch Smith)

Good friends of each other, Hogg and Peacock were excellent classical scholars. When Trelawny returned to England he became friends with both of them. It is significant that Greek references were used for coded communication on gay topics, not only by Byron and his friends (Crompton 1985), but also by Shelley and his friends. In a letter from Hogg to Shelley of 21 May 1820, we note the phrase, *noctes atticae* ("Attic nights"):

• The stepsister of Mary? (p. 30)
(his daughter-in-law (p151)

> Peacock has lately married, and in my opinion very judiciously; notwithstanding his *various* occupations, we sometimes find time for *noctes atticae,* or long walks. [emphases in original] (Shelley/Jones)

This is almost certainly related to the phrase, *the Attic Mode,* which Jeremy Bentham and his friends secretly used to refer to male love. (Crompton 2003) Peacock was a personal friend of Bentham, and Hogg was an intimate and life-long friend of a Bentham *protégé* and bachelor, Walter Coulson. (Scott 1951)

Peacock and Hogg also appear to use "Athenian" and "Greek" as code words for gay. (Scott 1943) The give-away is in a letter to Peacock, where Hogg mentions reading the *Erotes* of Lucian. (Scott) (The Lucian dialogue is a debate over heterosexual love versus pederasty, with the latter winning the contest.)

Peacock also came into his share of abuse from Jane, Lady Shelley. His offense was having defended the character of Shelley's first wife, Harriet, against the lies that Lady Shelley had published about her. As Peacock's facts and reasoning were irrefutable, she began disseminating the lie that Peacock had had an affair with Harriet. When Peacock's lawyers stopped her from doing this openly, she continued spreading the slander surreptitiously. On the whole, Jane Shelley was a sentimental, superstitious, bigoted, and unprincipled woman — who was fond of birds.

Who is this?

VIII. The Don Leon Poems

The *Don Leon* poems — *Don Leon: A Poem by Lord Byron* and *Leon to Annabella: An epistle from Lord Byron to Lady Byron* — are integral to a discussion of male love in the Shelley-Byron circle. These were first published in 1866, though both were probably written much earlier.

G. Wilson Knight, who rescued the poems from obscurity, insisted that *Don Leon* should be taken seriously from both a biographical and a literary standpoint. With regard to the poetry he asserted:

> However deeply we may be horrified by the subject, that does not excuse us from recognizing that the quality of the writing is of the highest order. Indeed, no such brilliant manipulation of the rhymed couplet has been known since Pope. (Knight 1957)

In addition to its biographical and literary values, *Don Leon* is of great interest as the first published polemic in English to argue for abolishing the sodomy ("buggery") statute. It begins by describing a man brought to the gallows, and then asks indignantly: "What had he done?" There follows a powerful attack against the brutality and stupidity of English legislation. Male love is vindicated through references to the mores and literature of classical antiquity.

Authorship of the poems is still a mystery. Despite the attribution, Byron could not have written *all* of the longer poem, *Don Leon,* since it refers to events that occurred after his death. Knight proposed the playwright, George Colman the Younger, as the author of *Don Leon,* partly on the basis of an underground attribution and partly on the basis of literary comparisons.

Louis Crompton regards Colman as an unlikely candidate on grounds of dating: Colman was elderly and ill in the 1830s, when *Don Leon* was probably written. He sums up the authorship issue as follows:

> Indeed, all we can say with certainty about the *Leon* poet is that he had a clever wit, a talent for writing forceful couplets, and a remarkable knowledge both of Byron's life (on its homosexual side) and of British parliamentary affairs in the decade following his death. (Crompton 1983)

However, it is not necessary to assume that both poems were written by a single author. Their quality is quite different: *Don Leon* is more forceful and polemical, whereas *Leon to Annabella* is more personal. And there is no reason why *Don Leon* could not represent a team effort. The copious notes, in several different languages, were obviously written by different hands over a long period of time.

In my opinion, the men in the Shelley-Byron circle are prime candidates, both individually and collectively, for authorship of the *Don Leon* poems. Byron could have written all of *Leon to Annabella* and Byron and Shelley could have written most of *Don Leon*; the rest of the latter could have been added by their friends after their deaths. But even if neither Byron nor Shelley had written a single line of the poems, the men who survived them were up to the task.

Peacock was a fine poet. Anyone who has read his *Rhododaphne*, written when he was in his thirties, knows that in maturity he would have had the technical skill to write the *Don Leon* couplets. Peacock's blistering attack on sexual cant in *Crochet Castle* has its counterpart in *Don Leon*.

Hogg had an analytical mind, wit, and a thorough knowledge of British legislation and parliamentary affairs. He had nerve, believed in sexual liberation, and knew how to collaborate. And he was a good friend of Peacock.

Trelawny was an excellent writer and a good thinker. His main contribution, however, would have been his daring and moral support. Think of the candor and conviction with which Trelawny describes his love for De Ruyter in *Adventures of a Younger Son*. (Appendix III) If Peacock or Hogg had shown any hesitation, he would have shaken it out of them. Trelawny had

° Not necessarily anti-religious, but certainly anti-christian. Poetry was their religion

known Byron intimately, and was a friend of both Peacock and Hogg.

Medwin should not be forgotten. Although his relations with Trelawny were occasionally strained, he was reconciled to him in the end. Like Trelawny, he had known Byron intimately. Like Peacock and Hogg, Medwin had a thorough knowledge of classical literature. In his Aeschylus translations he demonstrated his ability to write in powerful pentameter.

Conclusions

The full Shelley-Byron circle in Italy — Shelley, Byron, Medwin, Williams and Trelawny — lasted for only half a year before it was blown apart by the deaths of Shelley and Williams, the departure of Byron and Trelawny to fight for Greek independence, and the death of Byron. What were the characteristics of this group; and what goals, if any, did it have?

Male love was important to these men. It is significant that all of them were ardent Hellenists. Byron struck the note in Childe Harold's Pilgrimage to Greece: "Where'er we tread 'tis haunted, holy ground." All of them knew well that male love had flourished in Ancient Greece; the same male love that was persecuted their own time.

They were anti-religious,° with a particular hatred for Judeo-Christian sexual morality. Shelley's sentiment —

"Oh! I burn with impatience for the moment of Xtianity's dissolution, it has injured me; I swear on the altar of perjured love to revenge myself...." — was shared by the others. (1810 letter to Hogg)

They had a serious concern for justice. Given the character of these men, the daily meetings at Byron's palazzo would not have been all billiards and target shooting. They had goals. I believe that one of them was to work for the emancipation of male love. If so, they would have been forerunners of Heinrich Hössli, Karl Heinrich Ulrichs, John Addington Symonds, Sir Richard Burton, Edward Carpenter, the Scientific Humanitarian Committee, and the homophile and gay liberation movements of the 20th century. There may be little direct evidence to support this belief, but it fits in with what we know about them.

If so, were all of their efforts in vain? No doubt a great deal *was* lost, through the destruction of letters, memoirs, etc. But it is possible that some of their research, translations, and argumentation (if such there were) went into a Uranian underground to surface later in the works of others. As I have already argued, their efforts may have gone into *Don Leon.*

This story has had its ugly aspects: the destruction of documents — the suppression of masterpieces — the falsification of lives — the defamation of good people — the misinterpretation of great poems. The lesson is that we must rely on ourselves.

In 1921, nearly a century ago, the Action Committee of a gay united front in Germany declared: "In the final analysis, justice for you will be the fruit only of your own efforts. The liberation of homosexuals can only be the work of homosexuals themselves." (Lauritsen and Thorstad)

I would paraphrase this as, *the liberation of male love can only be the work of gay men.*

* * *

Edward John Trelawny in old age

Monument to Shelley by Weekes, commissioned by Jane, Lady Shelley. Modelled after Italian pietas, it portrays a dead Shelley as Jesus held by Mary as St. Mary.

Byron by George Henry Harlow, 1815

Thomas Jefferson Hogg at 65
Drawing by R. Easton

Edward Ellerker Williams,
Portrait by George Clint

John Keats drawn by his friend
Charles Armitage Brown

Byron by unknown artist
about time he left Harrow.

APPENDICES

APPENDIX I. Thomas Love Peacock.

The passage below is not only a marvelous example of high camp, but also a vigorous assault on sexual prudery.

A. *Crotchet Castle* (1831).

Excerpt from Chapter VII: "The Sleeping Venus":

There was an Italian painter, who obtained the name of *Il Bragatore,* [2] by the superinduction of inexpressibles [3] on the naked Apollos and Bacchuses of his betters. The fame of this worthy remained one and indivisible, till a set of heads, which had been, by a too common mistake of nature's journeymen, stuck upon magisterial shoulders, as the Corinthian capitals of 'fair round bellies with fat capon lined', but which nature herself had intended for the noddles of porcelain mandarins, promulgated simultaneously from the east and the west of

---

[2] Communication from Giovanni Dall'Orto, a gay historian living in Milano: "Peacock is surely referring to Daniele da Volterra, nicknamed 'il braghettone' (the 'inexpressibile' painter) for having veiled private parts in Michelangelo's Last Judgment. *Bragatore* is NOT an Italian word."

[3] *OED*: Inexpressible——B. sb. 2. pl. (colloq.) Breeches or trousers. (Orig. euphemistic....)

London, an order that no plaster-of-Paris Venus should appear in the streets without petticoats. Mr Crotchet, on reading this order in the evening paper, which, by the postman's early arrival, was always laid on his breakfast-table, determined to fill his house with Venuses of all sizes and kinds. In pursuance of this resolution, came packages by water-carriage, containing an infinite variety of Venuses. There were the Medicean Venus, and the Bathing Venus; the Uranian Venus, and the Pandemian Venus; the Crouching Venus, and the Sleeping Venus; the Venus rising from the sea, the Venus with the apple of Paris, and the Venus with the armour of Mars. [4]

The Reverend Doctor Folliott had been very much astonished at this unexpected display. Disposed, as he was, to hold, that whatever had been in Greece, was

---

[4] In this passage Peacock identifies the Pandemian Venus with immodesty ("naked") and the Uranian Venus with sexual modesty ("half-draped"). But Peacock, as an excellent classical scholar, knows there is more to it than this. In Plato's Dialogue on Love, *The Banquet* or *Symposium*, Pausanias postulates two gods of love: the Pandemian (Vulgar) Eros – son of the Pandemian Aphrodite (or Venus) – governs heterosexual or purely licentious relations, whereas the Uranian (Heavenly) Eros – son of the Uranian Aphrodite (or Venus) – governs principled male love: "This is that Love who attends on the Uranian deity, and is Uranian; the author of innumerable benefits both to the state and to individuals; and by the necessity of whose influence both the lover and the beloved are disciplined into the zeal of virtue." (Shelley translation)

Plato's Uranian Eros (or Love) by no means excludes sex between males; rather, he excludes relationships that are only licentious or promiscuous, as well as those that involve females.

right; he was more than doubtful of the propriety of throwing open the classical adytum to the illiterate profane.[5] Whether, in his interior mind, he was at all influenced, either by the consideration that it would be for the credit of his cloth, with some of his vice-suppressing neighbours, to be able to say that he had expostulated; or by curiosity, to try what sort of defence his city-bred friend, who knew the classics only by translation, and whose reason was always a little ahead of his knowledge, would make for his somewhat ostentatious display of liberality in matters of taste; is a question, on which the learned may differ: but, after having duly deliberated on two full-sized casts of the Uranian and Pandemian Venus, in niches on each side of the chimney, and on three alabaster figures, in glass cases, on the mantelpiece, he proceeded, peirastically,[6] to open his fire.

THE REV DR FOLLIOTT
These little alabaster figures on the mantelpiece, Mr Crotchet, and those large figures in the niches — may I take the liberty to ask you what they are intended to represent?

---

[5] "adytum". the innermost sanctuary or shrine in ancient temples which was open only to priests and from which oracles were given : a private chamber : SANCTUM, HOLY OF HOLIES. (Webster's *Third*)

[6] Peirastic. [Gk peirastikos, fr peiran to attempt] fitted for trial: experimental, tentative. (Webster's *Third*)

MR CROTCHET
Venus, sir; nothing more, sir; just Venus.

THE REV DR FOLLIOTT
May I ask you, sir, why they are there?

MR CROTCHET
To be looked at, sir; just to be looked at: the reason for most things in a gentleman's house being in it at all; from the paper on the walls, and the drapery of the curtains even to the books in the library, of which the most essential part is the appearance of the back.

THE REV DR FOLLIOTT
Very true, sir. As great philosophers hold that the esse of things is percipi, [7] so a gentleman's furniture exists to be looked at. Nevertheless, sir, there are some things more fit to be looked at than others; for instance, there is nothing more fit to be looked at than the outside of a book. It is, as I may say, from repeated experience, a pure and unmixed pleasure to have a goodly volume lying before you, and to know that you may open it if you please, and need not open it unless you please. It is a resource against ennui, if ennui should come upon you. To have the resource and not to feel the ennui, to enjoy your bottle in the present, and your book in the

---

[7] "*Esse est percipi*" (to be is to be perceived) is a dictum of George Berkeley (Bishop Berkeley, 1685-1753), an idealist philosopher.

indefinite future, is a delightful condition of human existence. There is no place, in which a man can move or sit, in which the outside of a book can be otherwise than an innocent and becoming spectacle. Touching this matter, there cannot, I think, be two opinions. But with respect to your Venuses there can be, and indeed there are, two very distinct opinions. Now, sir, that little figure in the centre of the mantelpiece, — as a grave paterfamilias, Mr Crotchet, with a fair nubile daughter, whose eyes are like the fish-pools of Heshbon, — I would ask you if you hold that figure to be altogether delicate? [8]

MR CROTCHET
The Sleeping Venus, sir? Nothing can be more delicate than the entire contour of the figure, the flow of the hair on the shoulders and neck, the form of the feet and fingers. It is altogether a most delicate morsel.

THE REV DR FOLLIOTT
Why, in that sense, perhaps, it is as delicate as whitebait in July. But the attitude, sir, the attitude.

MR CROTCHET
Nothing can be more natural, sir.

---

[8] "Thy neck is as a tower of ivory; thine eyes like the fish pools in Heshbon, by the gate of Bathrabbim; thy nose is as the tower of Lebanon which looketh toward Damascus." (*Song of Songs* 7:4)

THE REV DR FOLLIOTT

That is the very thing, sir. It is too natural: too natural, sir: it lies for all the world like — I make no doubt, the pious cheesemonger, who recently broke its plaster facsimile over the head of the itinerant vendor, was struck by a certain similitude to the position of his own sleeping beauty, and felt his noble wrath thereby justly aroused.

MR CROTCHET

Very likely, sir. In my opinion, the cheesemonger was a fool, and the justice who sided with him was a greater.

THE REV DR FOLLIOTT

Fool, sir, is a harsh term: call not thy brother a fool.

MR CROTCHET

Sir, neither the cheesemonger nor the justice is a brother of mine.

THE REV DR FOLLIOTT

Sir, we are all brethren.

MR CROTCHET

Yes, sir, as the hangman is of the thief; the 'squire of the poacher; the judge of the libeller; the lawyer of his client; the statesman of his colleague; the bubble-blower of the bubble-buyer; the slave-driver of the negro: as these are brethren, so am I and the worthies in question.

THE REV DR FOLLIOTT

To be sure, sir, in these instances, and in many others, the term brother must be taken in its utmost latitude of interpretation: we are all brothers, nevertheless. But to return to the point. Now these two large figures, one with drapery on the lower half of the body, and the other with no drapery at all; upon my word, sir, it matters not what godfathers and godmothers may have promised and vowed for the children of this world, touching the devil and other things to be renounced, if such figures as those are to be put before their eyes.

MR CROTCHET

Sir, the naked figure is the Pandemian Venus, and the half-draped figure is the Uranian Venus; and I say, sir, that figure realises the finest imaginings of Plato, and is the personification of the most refined and exalted feeling of which the human mind is susceptible; the love of pure ideal, intellectual beauty. [9]

[9] Later in the 19th century "Uranian" became a favored word of gay men in England. (Timothy d'Arch Smith 1970.) The 19th century Uranians, as well as Plato, understood that Uranian Love *did* include sex.

THE REV DR FOLLIOTT
I am aware, sir, that Plato, in his Symposium, discourseth very eloquently touching the Uranian and Pandemian Venus: but you must remember that, in our Universities Plato is held to be little better than a misleader of youth; and they have shown their contempt for him, not only by never reading him (a mode of contempt in which they deal very largely), but even by never printing a complete edition of him; although they have printed many ancient books which nobody suspects to have been ever read on the spot, except by a person attached to the press, who is therefore emphatically called 'the reader.' [10]

MR CROTCHET
Well, sir?

THE REV DR FOLLIOTT
Why, sir, to 'the reader' aforesaid (supposing either of our Universities to have printed an edition of Plato), or to any one else who can be supposed to have read Plato,

---

[10] During Peacock's lifetime, the only English translations of Plato's *Symposium* were bowdlerized. In order to conceal male love, the central theme of the dialogue, the translators reversed the genders, turning "him" into "her", and so on. Shelley's translation, which was known to Peacock, would have been the first in English to present the genders correctly; it was done in 1818 but only published complete and unbowdlerized over a century later — by Roger Ingpen in 1931. (Shelley 2001)

or indeed to be ever likely to do so, I would very willingly show these figures; because to such they would, I grant you, be the outward and visible signs of poetical and philosophical ideas: but, to the multitude, the gross carnal multitude, they are but two beautiful women, one half undressed, and the other quite so.

MR CROTCHET
Then, sir, let the multitude look upon them and learn modesty.

THE REV DR FOLLIOTT
I must say that, if I wished my footman to learn modesty, I should not dream of sending him to school to a naked Venus.

MR CROTCHET
Sir, ancient sculpture is the true school of modesty. But where the Greeks had modesty, we have cant; where they had poetry, we have cant; where they had patriotism, we have cant; where they had any thing that exalts, delights, or adorns humanity, we have nothing but cant, cant, cant. And, sir, to show my contempt for cant in all its shapes, I have adorned my house with the Greek Venus, [11] in all her shapes, and am ready to fight her

---

[11] Greek love (Greek Venus) – from Classical Antiquity to the present – means love between males, all-male sexuality. For example, *The Greeks and Greek Love* (2007) is the title of a book by James Davidson; its

battle against all the societies that ever were instituted for the suppression of truth and beauty. [12]

THE REV DR FOLLIOTT
My dear sir, I am afraid you are growing warm. Pray be cool. Nothing contributes so much to good digestion as to be perfectly cool after dinner.

****

B. Excerpt from *Memoirs of Percy Bysshe Shelley*, Fraser's Magazine, 1858:

Written by Peacock

This appetite for gossip about notorieties being once created in the "reading public", there will be always found persons to minister to it; and among the volunteers of this service, those who are best informed and who most valued the departed will probably not be the foremost. Then come biographies abounding with errors; and then, as matter of defence perhaps, comes on the part of friends a tardy and more authentic narrative. This is at best, as Mr Hogg describes it, a "difficult and delicate task". But it is always a matter of choice

---

meaning is immediately understood.

[12] A witty and powerful attack on sexual hypocrisy and Judeo-Christian sexual morality. It is not coincidental that Mr. Crochet's antagonist is a clergyman.

and discretion. No man is bound to write the life of another. No man who does so is bound to tell the public all he knows. On the contrary, he is bound to keep to himself whatever may injure the interests or hurt the feelings of the living, especially when the latter have in no way injured or calumniated the dead, and are not necessarily brought before the tribunal of public opinion in the character of either plaintiffs or defendants. Neither if there be in the life of the subject of the biography any event which he himself would willingly have blotted from the tablet of his own memory, can it possibly be the duty of a survivor to drag it into daylight. If such an event be the cardinal point of a life; if to conceal it or to misrepresent it would be to render the whole narrative incomplete, incoherent, unsatisfactory alike to the honour of the dead and the feelings of the living; then, as there is no moral compulsion to speak of the matter at all, it is better to let the whole story slumber in silence.

Having lived some years in very familiar intimacy with the subject of these memoirs; having had as good opportunities as any, and better than most persons now living, to observe and appreciate his great genius, extensive acquirements, cordial friendships, disinterested devotion to the well-being of the few with whom he lived in domestic intercourse, and ardent endeavours by private charity and public advocacy to ameliorate the condition of the many who pass their days in unremunerating toil; having been named his executor conjointly with Lord Byron, whose death, occurring before that of Shelley's father, when the son's will came into effect, left me alone in that capacity; having lived after his death in the same cordial intimacy with his widow, her family, and one or two at least of his surviving friends, I have been considered to have some peculiar advantages for writing his life, and have often been requested to do so; but for the reasons above given I have always refused.

[It has been asserted that the "event" alluded to by Peacock is Shelley's abandonment of his first wife, Harriet. However, Peacock never says this; and one is free to speculate that Shelley's love of other males is meant, which would come closer to being a "cardinal point" of his life.]

APPENDIX II. Percy Bysshe Shelley: *A Discourse on the Manners of the Antient [sic] Greeks Relative to The Subject of Love.*

Percy Bysshe Shelley wrote the essay below to accompany his translation of Plato's dialogue, *The Banquet* (*Symposium*). He felt that a stumbling block for readers would be the fact that male love lies at the heart of *The Banquet.*

Shelley's essay is only the second in English (after an unpublished 1785 essay by Jeremy Bentham) to address male-to-male sexuality. Unfortunately, it falls short of the mark. An over-wrought feminism leads Shelley to maintain that women in Ancient Greece were no better than slaves and that their degraded status caused males to turn to each other for amatory satisfaction. This is untenable because , in historical perspective, it is not male love which needs to be explained, but rather its condemnation — and the status of free women was not all that low.

Shelley questions what sexual techniques the Greeks used with each other and is "persuaded that it was totally different from the ridiculous and disgusting conceptions which the vulgar have formed on the subject." He means anal intercourse, and he goes into an extended diatribe against such a "detestable" violation of the beloved, one associated with "images of pain and horror." Here Shelley's ideas are in accord with many later writers — including Edward Carpenter, John

Addington Symonds, Havelock Ellis, and Andrew Calimach — who denied that the Greeks favored anal intercourse.

Shelley's description of his preferred sexual technique, the one he believes was favored by the Greeks, is necessarily non-specific. It would seem to involve bodily contact without penetration — perhaps what is known as *frottage* or the "Princeton rub". However, the most common male-to-male technique, according to surveys by Alfred Kinsey and Magnus Hirschfeld, is mutual masturbation, and no doubt the Greeks were familiar with it.

Although *Discourse* and translation were completed in 1818, they were first suppressed and then bowdlerized by Shelley's widow, Mary. Only in 1931, more than a century later, were they published complete and unexpurgated. —JL

****

The period which intervened between the birth of Pericles to the death of Aristotle, is undoubtedly, whether considered in itself or with reference to the effects which it had produced upon the subsequent destinies of civilised man, the most memorable in the history of the world. What was the combination of moral and political circumstances which produced so unparalleled a progress during that short period in literature and the arts; — why that progress, so rapid and so sustained, so soon received a check, and became retrograde, — are problems left with the wonder and conjectures of posterity. The wrecks and fragments of those subtle and profound minds, like the ruins of a fine statue, obscurely suggest to us the grandeur and perfection of the whole. Their very language — a type of the understandings of which it was the creation and the image — in variety, in simplicity, in flexibility, and in copiousness, excels every other language of the west-ern world. Their sculptures are such as we, in our pre-sumption, assume to be the models of ideal truth and beauty, and to which no artist of modern times can produce forms in any degree comparable. Their paint-ings, according to Pliny and Pausanias, were full of delicacy and harmony; and some even were powerfully pathetic, so as to awaken, like tender music or tragic poetry, the most overwhelming emotions. We are accustomed to conceive of the painters of the sixteenth century, as those who have brought their art to the highest perfection, probably because none of the an-cient paintings have been preserved. For all the inven-tive arts maintain, as it were, a sympathetic connection between each other, being no more than various ex-pressions of one internal power, modified by different circumstances, either of an individual, or of society; and the paintings of that period would probably bear the same relation as is confessedly borne by the sculptures to all succeeding ones. Of their music we know little; but the effects which it is said to have produced, whether they be attributed to the skill of the composer, or the sensibility of his audience, are far more powerful than any which we experience from the music of our own times; and if, indeed, the melody of their compositions were more tender and delicate, and inspiring, than the melodies of some modem European nations, their superiority in this art must have been something wonderful, and wholly beyond conception.

Their poetry seems also to maintain a very high, though not so disproportionate a rank, in the comparison. Perhaps Shakespeare, from the variety and comprehension of his genius, is to be considered, on a whole, as the greatest individual mind, of which we have specimens remaining. Perhaps Dante created imaginations of greater loveliness and energy than any that are to be found in the ancient literature of Greece. Perhaps nothing has been discovered in the fragments of the Greek lyric poets equivalent to the sublime and chivalric sensibility of Petrarch. — But, as a poet, Homer must be acknowledged to excel Shakespeare in the truth, the harmony, the sustained grandeur, the satisfying completeness of his images, their exact fitness to the illustration, and to that to which they belong. Nor could Dante, deficient in conduct, plan, nature, variety, and temperance, have been brought into comparison with these men, but for those fortunate isles, laden with golden fruit, which alone could tempt any one to embark in the misty ocean of his dark and extravagant fiction.

But, omitting the comparison of individual minds, which can afford no general inference, how superior was the spirit and system of their poetry to that of any other period! So that, had any genius equal in other respects to the greatest that ever enlightened the world, arisen in that age, he would have been superior to all, from this circumstance alone — that his conceptions would have assumed a more harmonious and perfect form. For it is worthy of observation, that whatever the poets of that age produced is as harmonious and perfect as possible. If a drama, for instance, were the composition of a person of inferior talent, it was still homogeneous and free from inequalities; it was a whole, consistent with itself. The compositions of great minds bore throughout the sustained stamp of their greatness. In the poetry of succeeding ages the expectations are often exalted on Icarean wings, and fall, too much disappointed to give a memory and a name to the oblivious pool in which they fell.

In physical knowledge Aristotle and Theophrastus had already — no doubt assisted by the labours of those of their predecessors whom they criticise — made [advances] worthy of the maturity of science. The astonishing invention of geometry, that series of discoveries which have enabled man to command the elements and foresee future events, before the subjects of his ignorant wonder, and has opened as it were the doors of the mysteries of nature, had already been brought to great perfection. Metaphysics, the science of man's intimate nature, and logic, or the grammar and elementary principles of that science, received from the latter philosophers of the Periclean age a firm basis. All our more exact philosophy is built upon the labours of these great men, and many of the words which we employ in metaphysical distinctions were invented by them to give accuracy and system to their reasonings. The science of morals, or the voluntary conduct of men in relation to themselves or others, dates from this epoch. How inexpressibly bolder and more pure were the doctrines of those great men, in comparison with the timid maxims which prevail in the writings of the most esteemed modern moralists. They were such as Phocion, and Epaminondas, and Timoleon, who formed themselves on their influence, were to the wretched heroes of our own age.

Their political and religious institutions were more difficult to bring into comparison with those of other times. A summary idea may be formed of the worth of any political and religious system, by observing the comparative degree of happiness and of intellect produced under its influence. And whilst many institutions and opinions, which in antient Greece were obstacles to the improvement of the human race, have been abolished among modern nations, how many pernicious superstitions and new contrivances of misrule, and unheard-of complications of public mischief, have not been invented among them by the ever-watchful spirit of avarice and tyranny!

The modern nations of the civilized world owe the progress which they have made — as well in those physical sciences in which they have already excelled their masters, as in the moral and intellectual enquiries, in which, with all the advantage of their experience of the latter, it can scarcely be said that they have yet equalled them, — to what is called the revival of learning; that is, the study of the writers of the age which preceded and immediately followed the government of Pericles, or of subsequent writers, who were, so to speak, the rivers flowing from those immortal fountains. And though there seems to be a principle in the modern world, which, should circumstances analogous to those which modelled the intellectual resources of the age to which we refer, into so harmonious a proportion, again arise, would arrest and perpetuate them, and consign their results to a more equal, extensive, and lasting improvement of the condition of man — though justice and the true meaning of human society is, if not more accurately, more generally understood; though perhaps men know more, and therefore are more, as a mass, yet this principle has never been called into action, and requires indeed a universal and almost appalling change in the system of existing things. The study of modern history is the study of kings, financiers, statesmen, and priests. The history of ancient Greece is the study of legislators, philosophers, and poets; it is the history of men, compared with the history of titles. What the Greeks were, was a reality, not a promise. And what we are and hope to be, is derived, as it were, from the influence and inspiration of these glorious generations.

Whatever tends to afford a further illustration of the manners and opinions of those to whom we owe so much, and who were perhaps, on the whole, the most perfect specimens of humanity of whom we have authentic record, were infinitely valuable. Let us see their errors, their weaknesses, their daily actions, their familiar conversation, and catch the tone of their society. When we discover how far the most admirable community ever formed, was removed from that perfection to which human society is impelled by some active power within each bosom, to aspire, how great ought to be our hopes, how resolute our struggles! For the Greeks of the Periclean Age were widely different from us. It is to [be] lamented that no modern writer has hitherto dared to show them precisely as they were. Barthélemy cannot be denied the praise of industry and system; but he never forgets that he is a Christian and a Frenchman. Wieland, in his delightful novels, makes indeed a very tolerable Pagan, but cherishes too many political preju-

° i.e. pederasty

dices, and refrains from diminishing the interest of his romances by painting sentiments in which no European of modern times can possibly sympathise. There is no book which shows the Greeks precisely as they were; they seem all written for children, with the caution that no practice or sentiment, highly inconsistent with our present manners, should be mentioned, lest those manners should receive outrage and violation. But there are many to whom the Greek language is inaccessible, who ought not to be excluded by this prudery to possess an exact and comprehensive conception of the history of man; for there is no knowledge concerning what man has been and may be, from partaking of which a person can depart, without becoming in some degree more philosophical, tolerant, and just.

One of the chief distinctions between the manners of ancient Greece and modern Europe, consisted in the regulations and the sentiments respecting sexual intercourse. Whether this difference arises from some imperfect influence of the doctrines of Jesus Christ, who alleges the absolute and unconditional equality of all human beings, or from the institutions of chivalry, or from a certain fundamental difference of physical nature existing in the Celts, or from a combination of all or any of these causes, acting on each other, is a question worthy of voluminous investigation. The fact is, that the modern Europeans have in this circumstance, and in the abolition of slavery, made an improvement the most decisive in the regulation of human society; and all the virtue and the wisdom of the Periclean age arose under other institutions, in spite of the diminution which personal slavery and the inferiority of women, recognized by law and by opinion, must have produced in the delicacy, the strength, the comprehensiveness, and the accuracy of their conceptions, in moral, political, and metaphysical science, and perhaps in every other art and science.

The women, thus degraded, became such as it was expected that they should become. They possessed, except with extraordinary exceptions, the habits and the qualities of slaves. They were probably not extremely beautiful; at least there was no such disproportion in the attractions of the external form between the female and male sex among the Greeks, as exists among the modern Europeans. They were certainly devoid of that moral and intellectual loveliness with which the acquisition of knowledge and the cultivation of sentiment animates, as with another life of overpowering grace, the lineaments and the gestures of every form which it inhabits. Their eyes could not have been deep and intricate from the workings of the mind, and could have entangled no heart in soul-enwoven labyrinths.

Let it not be imagined that because the Greeks were deprived of its legitimate object, they were incapable of sentimental love; and that this passion is the mere child of chivalry and the literature of modern times. This object, or its archetype, forever exists in the mind, which selects among those who resemble it, that which most resembles it; and instinctively fills up the interstices of the imperfect image, in the same manner as the imagination moulds and completes the shapes in clouds, or in the fire, into the resemblances of whatever form, animal, building, etc., happens to be present to it. Man is in his wildest state a social being: a certain degree of civilisation and refinement ever produces the want of sympathies still more intimate and complete; and the gratification of the senses is no longer all that is sought in sexual connection. It soon becomes a very small part of that profound and complicated sentiment, which we call Love, which is rather the universal thirst for a communion not merely of the senses, but of our whole nature, intellectual, imaginative and sensitive; and which, when individualized, becomes an imperious necessity, only to be satisfied by the complete or partial, actual or supposed, fulfilment of its claims. This want grows more powerful in proportion to the development which our nature receives from civilisation; for man never ceases to be a social being. The sexual impulse, which is only one, and often a small part of those claims, serves, from its obvious and external nature, as a kind of type or expression of the rest, as common basis, an acknowledged and visible link. Still it is a claim which even derives a strength not its own from the accessory circumstances which surround it, and one which our nature thirsts to satisfy. To estimate this, observe the degree of intensity and durability of the love of the male towards the female in animals and savages; and acknowledge all the duration and intensity observable in the love of civilised beings beyond that of savages to be produced from other causes. In the susceptibility of the external senses there is probably no important difference.

Among the ancient Greeks the male sex, one half of the human race, received the highest cultivation and refinement; whilst the other, so far as intellect is concerned, were educated as slaves, and were raised but few degrees in all that related to moral or intellectual excellence above the condition of savages. The gradations in the history of man present us with a slow improvement in this respect. The Roman women held a higher consideration in society, and were esteemed almost as the equal partners with their husbands in the regulation of domestic economy and the education of their children. The practices and customs of modern Europe are essentially different from and incomparably less pernicious than either, however remote from what an enlightened mind cannot fail to desire as the future destiny of human beings.

From this distinction arose that difference of manners which subsists between the antient Greeks and the modern Europeans. They both had arrived at that epoch of refinement, when sentimental love becomes an i.e. women

imperious want of the heart and of the mind. The senses of both sought with the same impatient eagerness that gratification upon which the perpetuity of our species depends. In modern Europe the sexual and intellectual claims of love, by the more equal cultivation of the two sexes, so far converge towards one point, as to produce, in the attempt to unite them, no gross violation in the established nature of man.

Among the Greeks these feelings, being thus deprived of their natural object, sought a compensation and a substitute. The men of Greece corresponded in external form to the models which they have left as specimens of what they were. The firm yet flowing proportion of their forms, the winning unreserve and facility of their manners, the eloquence of their speech, in a language which is itself music and persuasion; their gestures animated at once with the delicacy and the boldness which the perpetual habit of persuading and governing themselves and others; and the poetry of their religious rites, inspired into their whole being, rendered the youth of Greece a race of beings something widely different from that of modern Europe. If my observation be correct, the word καλος (beautiful) is more frequently applied to the male sex, whilst ευειδης (handsome) denoted the attractiveness of a female. Whether the cause is to be sought in the climate; in the original constitution of the peculiar race of the Greeks, or in the institutions and system of society, or in the mutual action of these several circumstances, such is the effect. And as a consequence of those causes, beautiful persons of the male sex became the object of that sort of feelings, which are only cultivated at present as towards females.

An enlightened philosophy, although it must condemn the laws by which an indulgence in the sexual instinct is usually regulated, suggests, however, the propriety of habits of chastity in like manner with those of temperance. It regards the senses as but a minute and subordinate portion of our complicated nature, and it deems the pleasures to be derived from their exercise as are weakened, not enhanced, by repetition, especially if unassociated with some principle from which they may participate, permanency and excellence. Few characters are more degraded than that of an habitual libertine; that is a person who is in the custom of seeking a relief from the impulse of the sexual instinct, divested of those associated sentiments which in a civilised state, precede, accompany, or follow such an act.

The act itself is nothing. The sources of condemnation to be pronounced against the indulgence in this gratification are twofold.

1st as it regards the complicated and arbitrary distinctions of society; and the other as it regards the indestructible laws of human nature.

With respect to the first, the one general law applicable to all other actions is applicable also to this: —

that nothing is to be done, which, including your own being in the estimate, will produce, on the whole, greater pain than pleasure. In this sense adultery, seductions, etc., until mankind shall have arrived... With respect to the second, the following propositions may be established as applications of this general law.

1st that the person selected as the subject of this gratification should be as perfect and beautiful as possible, both in body and in mind; so that all sympathies may be harmoniously blended, and the moments of abandonment be prepared by the entire consent of all the conscious portions of our being; the perfection of intercourse consisting, not perhaps in a total annihilation of the instinctive sense, but in the reducing it to as minute a proportion as possible, compared with those higher faculties of our nature, from which it derives a value.

2dly. Temperance in pleasure. This prevents the act which ought always to be the link and type of the highest emotions of our nature from degenerating into a diseased habit, equally pernicious to body and mind. Everyone will recollect Mrs Shandy's clock; and after the customary smile has past, cannot but be shocked at the picture it affords of the brutal prostitution of the most sacred impulses of our being.

3dly. This act ought to be indulged *according to nature.* A volume of definitions and limitations belong to this maxim, which here may be passed over.

To apply these propositions to the Greeks. The passion which their poets and philosophers described and felt seems inconsistent with this latter maxim, in a degree inconceivable to the imagination of a modern European. But let us not exaggerate the matter. We are not exactly aware, — and the laws of modern composition scarcely permit a modest writer to investigate the subject with philosophical accuracy, — what that action was by which the Greeks expressed this passion. I am persuaded that it was totally different from the ridiculous and disgusting conceptions which the vulgar have formed on the subject, at least except among the more debased and abandoned of mankind. It is impossible that a lover could usually have subjected the object of his attachment to so detestable a violation or have consented to associate his own remembrance in the beloved mind with images of pain and horror. If we consider the facility with which certain phenomena connected with sleep, at the age of puberty, associate themselves with those images which are the objects of our waking desires; and even that in some persons of an exalted state of sensibility, that a similar process may take place in reverie, it will not be difficult to conceive the almost involuntary consequences of a state of abandonment in the society of a person of surpassing attractions, when the sexual connection cannot exist, to be such as to preclude the necessity of so operose and diabolical a machination as that usually described. This is the result apparently alluded to by Plato. That it could seldom have approached to a resemblance with the vulgar imputation, even among the more gross and unrefined Romans, I appeal to a passage of Petronius, well known to every scholar, in which Giton, the pathic is represented to talk the language of a woman receiving pleasure from the embraces of Encolpius. This, even as a piece of meretricious flattery, is wholly inconsistent with the vulgar notion.

But let us not measure the Greeks of the age to which I refer, with our own feeble conceptions of the intensity of disinterested love; or according to the horrible commentary which the imitation of their manners by the licentious Romans, who had contributed to the overthrow of the Republic, produced upon the text. Probably there were innumerable instances among that exalted and refined people, in which there never happened any circumstance between the lover and his beloved by which natural modesty was wronged. The lover appeased his physical instinct with his wife or his slave; or was engrossed in such lofty thoughts and feelings as admitted of no compromise between them and less intense emotions. Thus much is to be admitted, that, represent this passion as you will, there is something totally irreconcilable in its cultivation to the beautiful order of social life, to an equal participation in which all human beings have an indefeasible claim, and from which half of the human race, by the Greek arrangement, were excluded. This invidious distinction of human kind, as a class of beings [of] intellectual nature, into two sexes, is a remnant of savage barbarism which we have less excuse than they for not having totally abolished.

The action by which this passion was expressed, taken in its grossest sense, is indeed sufficiently detestable. But a person must be blinded by superstition to conceive of it as more horrible than the usual intercourse endured by almost every youth of England with a diseased and insensible prostitute. It cannot be more unnatural, for nothing defeats and violates nature, or the purposes for which the sexual instincts are supposed to have existed, than prostitution. Nor is it possible that the society into which the one plunges its victim should be more pernicious than the other. Nothing is at the same time more melancholy and ludicrous than to observe that the inhabitants of one epoch, or of one nation, harden themselves to all amelioration of their own practices and institutions and soothe their consciences by heaping violent invectives upon those of others; while in the eye of sane philosophy their own are no less deserving of censure. If it be enquired how an individual ought to act — the reply is — make the best of a bad matter.

The ideas suggested by Catullus, Martial, Juvenal and Suetonius never occur among the Greeks; nor even among those Romans, who, like Lucretius, Virgil and

Horace, imitated them. The Romans were brutally obscene; the Greeks seemed hardly capable of obscenity in a strict sense. How innocent is even the "Lysistrata" of Aristophanes compared with the infamous perversions of Catullus! The earlier dramatic English writers are often frightfully obscene, exceeding even the Romans. I should consider obscenity to consist in a capability of associating disgusting images with the act of the sexual instinct. Luxury produced for the Romans what the venereal disease did for the writers of James, and after the redeeming interval over which Milton presided the effects of both were united, under Charles II, to infect literature.

It may blunt the harshness of censure also to reflect that in the golden age of our own literature a certain sentimental attachment towards persons of the same sex was not uncommon. Shakespeare has devoted the impassioned and profound poetry of his sonnets to commemorate an attachment of this kind, which we cannot question was wholly divested of any unworthy alloy. Towards the age of Charles II it is said that this romantic friendship degenerated into licentiousness. The latter age bears the same relation to the former as the first of the Roman Empire, to [the Republic].

Thus far the translator has thought it his duty to overstep the jealous limits between what the learned and the unlearned know of the Greeks; and to indicate a system of reasoning which may enable the reader to form a liberal, consistent, and just judgement of the peculiarities of their domestic manners. This slight sketch was undertaken to induce the reader to cast off the cloak of his self-flattering prejudices and forbid the distinction of manners, which the author has endeavoured to preserve in the translation of the ensuing piece, to interfere with his delight or his instruction.

This essay unfortunately does not shed any real light on the Symposium. As an introduction to the dialogue it is useless.

APPENDIX III. Edward John Trelawny.

A. *Adventures of a Younger Son,* A new edition with an introduction by Edward Garnett, T. Fisher Unwin, London 1890. Originally published in 1831.

Excerpt from Chapter CXIX:

[Trelawny recalls his love for a young officer he had known only briefly.]

As a neutral vessel lay in the port, we shipped Darvell, and the men we had rescued, on board her. Both De Ruyter and myself parted from that gallant young officer with deep regret. In those days of my youth my heart was glowing with feeling, and, as has been seen, readily formed alliances with noble minds like Darvell's. Such men as he, (though I cannot believe there are many,) may still live; and perhaps, occasionally, I may come unknowingly in contact with them; but my heart is chilled, and my affections almost extinguished. I no longer feel myself moved to claim kindred with them; my soul is absorbed in selfish and vain regret for those I have loved and lost, and shrinks from new ties, if not with loathing, yet with cold indifference. I am become ascetic and morbid; so I will not slander human nature by contrasting Darvell and the friends of my youth, such as they were to me, with the worldlings among whom I now associate, and whom, with sneering mockery, I designate as "dear," on every scrap of paper which necessity compels me to address to them, either for the purpose of an invitation to dinner, or an appointment for a duel. Let me, however, although no verbal critic, protest against the profanation of the word friend. In this my history I must be honest, make a distinction between the oriental diamond and its worthless imitation of paste, and separate the grain from the chaff — gossamer words, that weigh nothing, from substantial realities heavier than gold. With heartfelt reluctance I parted with Darvell, and it is painful for me now to dismiss him with so faint an outline as I have traced on this paper.

Excerpt from Chapter XV:

[Trelawny is a boy of seventeen in the British Navy in a port city somewhere in the Indian Ocean. Here he meets De Ruyter, a man of twenty-nine.]

At the tavern where I took up my abode, I commenced an intimacy with a merchant. In youth we form friendship in days, which, at a more advanced age, require years. So with this man; from a game or two at billiards, eating together, and walking together, we had become boon companions. Many of the naval officers used to come in parties to the tavern to see me, when we often sallied about the town, and played a thousand mad pranks. My friend, the stranger, as he was called, seemed to seek the society of naval officers, and take great interest in the different accounts of their cruises, the ships they belonged to, their rate of sailing, and the peculiarities which distinguished their respective commanders. His conversation was principally confined to questions, and, as people, for the most part, prefer talking to listening, he was liked the better. He frequently, in company with me, visited the men-of-war in the harbour; the only one I objected to introduce him to was my own frigate, but to make him amends, I gave every information he wished regarding her.

Though he then called himself De Witt, I shall speak of him at once under his real name, De Ruyter. He mentioned to me that he was waiting for a passage to Batavia; he seemed perfectly acquainted with India and its seas. He spoke most of the European languages, nor had he the slightest foreign accent in his pronunciation of the English. In walking about the bazars, commonly at night, he sometimes met me, and took me with him. He was familiar with all the out-of-the-way corners of the most irregular of towns, and entered into many dark abodes without ceremony. He conversed, on these occasions, with the natives, in their varied tongues with equal ease, whether in the guttural, brute-like grunting of the Malay, the more humanized Hindostanee, or the softer and harmonious Persian. What struck me most at the time, was, the great deference these people paid him; even the proud, fat, swelling, and pompous Armenian merchants stopped their palanquins, and got out to converse with him, apparently delighted at their meeting. These and other circumstances made me wonder, but nothing more; at seventeen we do not expect every man to be a rogue as we do at thirty. There was a self-possession and decision about De Ruyter's ordinary acts, with a general information, that made me feel what, I suppose, I should not have thanked any one for remarking, as, at that age, we are loth to allow any to be our superior. Perhaps I might not have felt this so strongly, had he not been as much my superior in physical as in mental endowments. In stature he was majestic, the length and fine proportion of his limbs, and the shortness and roundness of his body, gave to his appearance a lightness and elasticity seldom seen but in the natives of the east. It was only on close examination you discovered, that under the slim form of the date-tree was disguised the solid strength of the oak. His face wanted breadth to please an artist's eye, but it added to the effect of his high, clear, bold, unwrinkled forehead, as smooth, though not as white, as sculptured marble. His hair was dark and abundant, his features well defined. The greatest peculiarity was his eye; it was ever so varying that it was impossible to distinguish its colour; like the hue of the cameleon it had no fixed tint, but shewed, as in a mirror, the reflection of his mind. In a state of rest it was overcast with a hazy film, like a grey cloud; but when he was excited by the vehemence of his feelings, the mist evaporated, and it gradually brightened, till its rays, like the sun, became so intense, that your own were dazzled beholding it.

His eye-lashes were jet-black; he had thick, straight, and prominent eye-brows, with a habit of knitting them together, contracted from exposure to the intense heat of an eastern sun, leaving an infinity of minuter lines, traced at the corners of the eyes, but unlike the deep furrows of age or debauchery in northern climates. The lines of his mouth were boldly and clearly cut; it was muscular, full of expression, and the upper lip, which was prominent, had a convulsive action when he spoke, independent of its companion; his jaw was full, and gave him the air of invincible determination. Though naturally not of so dark a complexion as myself, those parts of his person exposed were not merely sun-burnt, but appeared to be seared to the very bone. He was approaching his thirtieth year.

I am thus minute in describing De Ruyter, to account in part for the extraordinary influence he gained, on so short an acquaintance, over my mind and imagination. He became my model. The height of my ambition was to imitate him, even in his defects. My emulation was awakened. For the first time I was impressed with the superiority of a human being. To keep on an equality with him was unattainable. In every trifling action he evinced a manner so off-hand, free, and noble, that it looked as if it sprung new and fresh from his own individuality; and every thing else shrunk into an apish imitation.

Excerpt from Chapter LIX:

[Port St. Louis in Mauritius, an island in the southwest Indian Ocean. The teenaged Trelawny, in Arab costume, is ushered into the dressing room of the wife of the French commandant.]

She made me sit by her on the couch, and asked me all sorts of questions, never doubting I was not what I seemed. She told me I was handsome, and my shawls were handsomer, wished to know if they came from Cashmire, why I shaved my head, if I believed in the Virgin Mary, if I had ever loved, and if I would be christened. Her hands kept pace with her tongue till she almost stripped me to examine my apparel. My skin, she said, was very smooth, not very black, and she asked if Arab women were handsome, and if I liked the French women. Then she told me she was returning shortly to France, because she could no longer endure the heat, the barbarous people, the want of society, the want of an opera, of every necessary of life, — except the real ones, which she allowed were good and abundant, — but these she did not want. Here she was interrupted by De Ruyter, a great favourite of hers. She called him the only real gentleman on the island, as he had passed many of his early years in France and at Paris. Upon which she talked unceasingly of Paris. "Dear De Ruyter," she said, "does this boy belong to you? Where did you get him? I have taken a great fancy to him, and positively I am determined to take him to Paris. Only think what a sensation he will make there! Well! it is wonderful these people, who live on the sands, with the lions and tigers, should have such a distinguished air, and carry themselves so well! And then, my dear De Ruyter, only think what he will be when he has passed a winter in Paris, and learnt to waltz! Well, you are a dear creature, — and remember you have given him to me. How beautifully he puts on his turban, and — what is your name? Come, shew me how you fold your turban. Everyone in Paris will be dying in love with — your turban and shawls."

She ran on in this style till wearied; then vowing I should remain with her, and that she could not bear me out of her presence an instant, she threw herself on a couch, and pointed to me to get a punka and fan. "Ah! who would live here," she ejaculated, "where the heat is so insufferable that a person cannot say a single word of welcome to an old friend, without being ready to expire!"

[The lady wants Trelawny and De Ruyter to sleep over during the heat of the day, but they make their escape.]

Excerpt from Chapter LX:

[De Ruyter and Trelawny return home after visiting the French commandant and his wife. De Ruyter is jealous of the woman's attentions to Trelawny and also of Trelawny's child bride, Zela. He goes into a long diatribe.]

"... Poor boy, I pity you I for I see you have resigned yourself, a willing slave, to the worst and most enervating of human passions. Women are like parasitical plants, casting their wild tendrils from one tree to another, till, swollen into tough cordage, they strangle those they embrace, and luxuriate in their decay. That broad and open forehead indicates a judgment, which, when matured to fulness, ought, with its iron grasp, to crush the reptile passion, soon as it has birth. Men like you are for nobler uses, for actions that may benefit mankind, not to be dedicated to the narrow, paltry, selfish views and gratifications of a solitary individual, however worthy. What! devote yourself to the childish pastime of fondling a tawdry toy, a baby's doll!" Seeing me silent and sad, he ended by quoting his favourite authority, on all questions, but, like all others, quoting only for his own purpose:

Rouse yourself; and the weak wanton Cupid
Shall from your neck unloose his amorous fold,
And, like a dew-drop from the lion's mane,
Be shook to air.

Soon after he added, by way of softening the pain his taunts had given me, "I do not mean to censure you for loving Zela. She is your wife, dependent on you, and most worthy to be loved. But I object to your exclusively loving her, and withdrawing your affections from others, together with your time and talents which can be beneficially employed."

[The quotation from Shakespeare's Troilus and Cressida is a dead giveaway that the relationship between De Ruyter and Trelawny is sexual. Following is the full passage, in which Patroclus addresses Achilles:

To this effect, Achilles, have I mov'd you.
A woman impudent and mannish grown
Is not more loath'd than an effeminate man
In time of action. I stand condemn'd for this;
They think my little stomach to the war
And your great love to me restrains you this.
Sweet, rouse yourself; and the weak wanton Cupid
Shall from your neck unloose his amorous fold,
And like a dew-drop from the lion's mane,
Be shook to airy air.

[It is revealing that Trelawny should be intimately familiar with the only Shakespeare play to make explicit reference to all-male sexuality. Achilles and Patroclus are clearly shown to be lovers; Patroclus is derided by Thersites, a fool and a slanderer, as "Achilles' male varlet" and his "masculine whore".]

Excerpt from Chapter CXXIX:

[Trelawny's anguished parting from De Ruyter, who was killed several months later in the service of Napoleon.]

I am totally unable to write what I felt when the moment arrived which was to separate me from the man I loved better, a thousand times, than ever before one man could love another. The sun was setting, and the night must have been cold, for my limbs shook, and I could hardly support myself. I was obliged to hold on the iron rail of the stone steps, leading from the quay to the boat in which I was to embark. When we had descended, to be in a line with the boat, I was insensible to the water, which worked up to my knees. Exhausted as if I had run a race, yet my movements were solemn as the chief mourner at a funeral. De Ruyter also was touched; his bronzed face was of a leaden hue; though I believe he talked calmly and distinctly, I could not afterwards remember a word he had said, but, "Farewell, my dear boy!" Then, with an effort to speak more cheerfully, he added the consolatory words, "In six months we meet again!"

His hand waved a last farewell! My heart — I thought nothing more could move it — swelled to bursting; and my eyelids which, since Zela's death, had been dry and hot, became moist. The heart is the organ of true wisdom, gifted with prophetic power; it looks into futurity. Though De Ruyter's words were, "We shall meet again," a prediction so rational to the judgment that mine could not gainsay it; yet my heart, never before doubting that what he averred must be, now refused to register what he said — it added to his words, "Farewell for ever!"

What could I but cling to De Ruyter? Like one suspended over a cliff by a single rope, I held him; and the feelings that overcame me at parting were as seeing that rope giving way, or as, with more appalling agony, a sailor fallen into the sea at midnight, catching the last glimpse of his ship, his limbs paralysed, his swelling heart bursts. I am one whose faith is, that love and friendship, with ardent natures, are like those trees of the torrid zone which yield fruit but once, and then die.

****

B. *Records of Shelley, Byron, and the Author.*

Excerpt from Chapter 9:

[An intimate conversation among three young men — Trelawny, Percy Bysshe Shelley, and Edward Ellerker Williams — "pariahs" living in Italy. Although the reasons for their "exile" (Shelley) are never explicitly given, one should remember that in their native land, England, men and boys were regularly being hanged for having sex with each other — but in Italy, thanks to the Code Napoléon, sex between males was legal.]

One day as the sun was setting, and I was crossing from the south to the north side of the bridge at Pisa, I ran against Williams; and, a few minutes after, caught sight of Shelley's bright eyes in the distance.... *[The three of them begin a dialogue.]*

TRELAWNY: As we three castaways have met from three crossroads, we should sit down here, open our wallets, and, when we are refreshed, tell our stories in the fashion of the old wayfarers and pilgrims. We are three birds of the same feather, same age (twenty-nine), were cast out at about the same time, and denounced as Pariahs. We are more than one thousand miles from the island we were hatched in; our affectionate parents hove us out of our nests as the birds heave their young out of theirs, on this dangerous earth. How we escaped from the ground-vermin, reptiles, and traps, and gained strength to take this long flight, we must now tell. You, Williams, will find bread in Shelley's wallet; I will dull my senses with a cigar. Neither of you has ever used the noxious weed; to me it's a solace. As Shelley says he is three times as old as either of us, he must first recount his adventures

SHELLEY: Mine is a life of failures. Peacock says my poetry is composed of day-dreams and nightmares; and Leigh Hunt does not think it good enough for the Examiner. Jefferson Hogg says all poetry is inverted sense, and consequently nonsense. Every man should attempt to do something. Poetry was the rage of the day, and I racked my imagination to be a poet. I wrote, and the critics denounced me as a mischievous visionary, and my friends said that I had mistaken my vocation, that my poetry was mere rhapsody of words; that I was soaring in the blue regions of the air, disconnected from all human sympathy. I should have liked to be a sailor; Tre says I cannot.

WILLIAMS: Why?

TRELAWNY: Because he cannot smoke, or drink, or swear, and those are essential qualifications for a sailor.

APPENDIX IV. Thomas Jefferson Hogg, *The Life of Percy Bysshe Shelley.*

Shelley seldom observed peculiarities of dress, but there was amongst these unfortunates an old fellow, he was a French duke, I believe, whose costume was so extraordinary that even he noticed it, and laughed heartily at the strange disguise. My Lord, the duke, was strongly possessed by Anglomania, which he continued to indulge, although he was paying so dearly for it in purse and in person, and for his countrymen's love of constitutional freedom. He was particularly ambitious to dress exactly like an Englishman, so that he might be taken for one, and after divers failures, he succeeded at last completely. This was his type; the purely English, or Anglomaniacal, habit was this. His coat was of cloth, of that kind of grey called pepper and salt, very light, indeed, much salt, with very little pepper. The waistcoat was of pepper and salt also, hut darker, with more pepper. His shorts were of a like material, the pepper predominating, and therefore being darker than the waistcoat; and his long gaiters were still darker, the darkest of all, being almost entirely pepper, with scarcely any salt.

We were ushered one morning into a room, where this figure of fun was sitting alone. After sundry profound reverences and an exhortation not to despair, for our friends, he was assured and could assure us, would soon appear, he gravely asked me, if he did not look exactly like an Englishman? If I could possibly suspect that he was a foreigner, a Frenchman? "My lord, the duke, does us a very great honour in desiring so much to resemble us, and so closely!" My answer was accepted by the Anglomaniac as altogether satisfactory; but Bysshe broke forth into a shrieking peal of laughter, and rushed headlong out of the room.

"Is your friend taken ill, sir?"

"He is afflicted with a spasmodic cough".

"Poor fellow! Poor young man!"

And the good-natured, unsuspecting peer seriously recommended that Eau de Luce should be frequently rubbed on his chest by a soft, warm hand.

"Eau de Luce is easily procured, but where will he find the soft, warm hand?"

"Oh! with his truly charming physiognomy, he will very easily find that!"

I repeated the gracious and graceful compliment to the culprit with the deserved warning:

"If you laugh at the poor old fellow's fashionable English suit again, you will be an ingrate, a thorough wretch! I will not shelter you any more...." [pp. 498-499]

APPENDIX V. *Epipsychidion.*

Epipsychidion (1822) is one of Shelley's most problematic poems. A dream-like meditation on ideal love, it espouses Free Love, ridicules the chains of monogamy, and suggests that his lovers could be either female or male.

Shelley's dedication reads: "Verses addressed to the noble and unfortunate Lady, Emilia, ———— now imprisoned in the convent of————." This refers to Countess Emilia Viviani, a young woman residing in the Convent of St. Anna, whom Shelley visited a few times and with whom he corresponded briefly.

Although many lines of *Epipsychidion* appear to be addressed to "Emilia", this may be a red herring. Despite the overactive imagination of Shelley's biographers, there is not the slightest reason to believe that he had an amorous interest in Emilia — never once did he visit her without being chaperoned by his wife and/or Claire Clairmont.

Epipsychidion is a cryptic poem, a *poèm à clef.* Critics have speculated whether Mary Shelley is symbolized by "moon", Claire Clairmont by "comet", and so on. Shelley makes it clear in his preface to the poem, labelled as an "Advertisement", that he is posing puzzles and dealing in mystification. The poem's meaning will be "sufficiently intelligible to a certain class of readers", but "incomprehensible" to others. Who are those intended readers? Shelley indicated in a letter to his publisher, Ollier, that he desired *Epipsychidion* to be circulated only to the *sunetoi* (the initiated, the *cognoscenti*, the enlightened, the "esoteric few" [Shelley's words]). That gay men might represent Shelley's "certain class of readers" or *sunetoi* is as reasonable as any other conjecture.

After 406 cryptic lines, with occasional appeals to "Emilia", the poem suddenly changes character with a line break and an appeal to "Emily". The section that follows, addressed to "Emily" rather than "Emilia", is almost two hundred lines of beautiful and erotic poetry. I suggest the possibility that "Emily" is not a variant of "Emilia", but stands for Edward Ellerker Williams — Shelley's beloved companion — either as a code name for him or as his nickname. (The men in the Shelley-Byron circle did use feminine nicknames for each other, for example, "Polly" for John Polidori. Shelley and Williams met in early January 1821, over a month before the *Epipsychidion* manuscript was sent to the printer.

Alternatively, "Emily" may stand for some other male love of Shelley's, or even an imagined and idealized male love. Shelley may have had, and probably did have, love affairs about which we know nothing. This is to be expected: most people, who exercise a modicum of discretion, succeed in keeping their private love lives hidden. In Shelley's case, we should never forget the efforts of his widow, Mary, and his daughter-in-law,

Jane, Lady Shelley, to create a myth, to turn him into "a Victorian angel suitable for enshrinement among the gods of respectability and convention." (Smith) Considering the massive destruction of letters, manuscripts, and journal entries by Mary and Jane Shelley, a lack of evidence means nothing. We can only imagine what they destroyed.

Throughout the final, "Emily" section of *Epipsychidion* are references to sailing, which Shelley and Williams enjoyed from the time they met until the time they died together, a year and a half later — references to the mutual attraction of equals — references to soul mates, the myth of Aristophanes. Despite the "lord/lady" terms, the concluding episode resonates with those qualities that are inherent in an all-male relationship.

Some additional lines, which did not appear in print, were found and printed in 1903 by C.D. Locock; these were then included in the standard edition of Shelley's *Poetical Works* edited by Thomas Hutchinson. Some of these additional lines are merely rejects, but others are very fine and highly revealing. Shelley indicates that male love is at least a major theme of the poem; that he must "veil" the gender of his "friend"; that he is using trickery, concealment and camouflage. In light of these additional lines, gender cannot simply be assumed: "lady" may really mean "lord" and "she" may mean "he". Anything is possible.

In four highly revealing lines Shelley declares that he has a friend who is also a lover, and that those who are too obtuse to recognize this might find a clue in Shakespeare's sonnets — in which an older man expresses his love for a beautiful younger man:

> If any should be curious to discover
> Whether to you I am a friend or lover,
> Let them read Shakespeare's sonnets, taking thence
> A whetstone for their dull intelligence....

The ending of *Epipsychidion,* beginning with "Emily / A ship is floating in the harbour now....", makes perfect sense if it is addressed to Williams, his friend and sailing companion; it makes very little sense addressed to a young woman in a convent.

Below are the following: 1) an excerpt from Shelley's "Advertisement for Epipsychidion", 2) lines 408-591 of *Epipsychidion,* with footnote annotation to explicate homoerotic references. and 3) the "Passages of the poem, or connected therewith", which were not printed with *Epipsychidion,* also with footnote annotation.

ADVERTISEMENT

The Writer of the following lines died at Florence, as he was preparing for a voyage to one of the wildest of the Sporades, which he had bought, and where he had fitted up the ruins of an old building, and where it was his hope to have realised a scheme of life, suited perhaps to that happier and better world of which he is now an inhabitant, but hardly practicable in this. His life was singular; less on account of the romantic vicissitudes which diversified it, than the ideal tinge which it received from his own character and feelings. The present Poem, like the Vita Nuova of Dante, is sufficiently intelligible to a certain class of readers without a matter-of-fact history of the circumstances to which it relates; and to a certain other class it must ever remain incomprehensible, from a defect of a common organ of perception for the ideas of which it treats....

****

Epipsychidion

Lines 408-591:

Emily, [13]
A ship is floating in the harbour now,
A wind is hovering o'er the mountain's brow;
There is a path on the sea's azure floor,
No keel has ever plough'd that path before;
The halcyons brood around the foamless isles; [14]

---

[13] Or Edward. In a fragment connected to *Epipsychidion*, Shelley indicates that he must veil the person to whom *Epipsychidion* is addressed: "What you are is a thing that I must veil." (Shelley 1970, p. 426.) If, as seems most likely from the context of these fragments, Shelley veiled the gender of his love object, then "Emily" could be read as "Edward" – his beloved companion, Edward Ellerker Williams.

Shelley indicated in a letter to his publisher, Ollier, that he desired *Epipsychidion* to be circulated only to the *sunetoi* (the initiated, the *cognoscenti*, the enlightened, the "esoteric few" [Shelley's words]). He may also have circulated to his sunetoi, either through himself or through Ollier, a key to *Epipsychidion*, indicating that "Emily" should be read as "Edward", and that masculine words should be substituted for feminine – for example, "heart's sister" should be read as "heart's brother", "lady" as "lord", and so on. In terms of metrics, the masculine words read just as well.

Alternatively, "Emily" may be Edward's nickname. (Like many gay men, the men in the Shelley-Byron circle did use feminine nicknames for each other, for example, "Polly" for Dr. John Polidori.)

[14] "Halcyon". In Greek legend, a fabled bird with the power to calm the wind and waves while nesting at sea during the winter solstice. As adjective: calm and peaceful, prosperous, golden.

The treacherous Ocean has forsworn its wiles;
The merry mariners are bold and free:
Say, my heart's sister, wilt thou sail with me? [15]
Our bark is as an albatross, whose nest
Is a far Eden of the purple East;
And we between her wings will sit, while Night,
And Day, and Storm, and Calm, pursue their flight,
Our ministers, along the boundless Sea,
Treading each other's heels, unheededly.
It is an isle under Ionian skies, [16]
Beautiful as a wreck of Paradise, [17]
And, for the harbours are not safe and good,
This land would have remain'd a solitude
But for some pastoral people native there,
Who from the Elysian, clear, and golden air [18]
Draw the last spirit of the age of gold,

---

[15] "heart's sister". If gender is veiled, then "heart's sister" would really be "heart's brother". This is one of many references to the "soul of my soul" or soul mate.

[16] "Ionian". Referring to "a Hellenic people of Mycenaean origin that inhabited Attica, the Peloponnesus along the Saronic Gulf." (*American Heritage Dictionary*, hereafter *AHD*) Note that in Jeremy Bentham's circle, which overlapped the Shelley-Byron circle, "attic mode" was a code expression for gay, homosexual. (Crompton 1985)

[17] Compare "Lost Angel of a ruined Paradise!" – referring to John Keats in Shelley's poem *Adonais*.

[18] "Elysian". Referring to the Elysian Fields – in Greek mythology, the abode of the blessed.

Simple and spirited; innocent and bold.
The blue Aegean girds this chosen home, [19]
With ever-changing sound and light and foam,
Kissing the sifted sands, and caverns hoar;
And all the winds wandering along the shore
Undulate with the undulating tide:
There are thick woods where sylvan forms abide;
And many a fountain, rivulet and pond,
As clear as elemental diamond,
Or serene morning air; and far beyond,
The mossy tracks made by the goats and deer
(Which the rough shepherd treads but once a year)
Pierce into glades, caverns and bowers, and halls
Built round with ivy, which the waterfalls
Illumining, with sound that never fails
Accompany the noonday nightingales;
And all the place is peopled with sweet airs;
The light clear element which the isle wears
Is heavy with the scent of lemon-flowers,
Which floats like mist laden with unseen showers,
And falls upon the eyelids like faint sleep;
And from the moss violets and jonquils peep
And dart their arrowy odour through the brain

---

[19] "Aegean". The Aegean Sea is a branch of the Mediterranean Sea off southeast Europe between Greece and Turkey. Still another reference to Ancient Greece. Whether intentional or not, the iteration of Greek references, in a passage of erotic love poetry, inevitably suggests Greek Love, or love between males.

Till you might faint with that delicious pain.
And every motion, odour, beam and tone,
With that deep music is in unison:
Which is a soul within the soul -- they seem [20]
Like echoes of an antenatal dream.
It is an isle 'twixt Heaven, Air, Earth and Sea,
Cradled and hung in clear tranquillity;
Bright as that wandering Eden Lucifer, [21]
Wash'd by the soft blue Oceans of young air.
It is a favour'd place. Famine or Blight,
Pestilence, War and Earthquake, never light
Upon its mountain-peaks; blind vultures, they
Sail onward far upon their fatal way:
The wingèd storms, chanting their thunder-psalm
To other lands, leave azure chasms of calm
Over this isle, or weep themselves in dew,
From which its fields and woods ever renew
Their green and golden immortality.
And from the sea there rise, and from the sky
There fall, clear exhalations, soft and bright,
Veil after veil, each hiding some delight,
Which Sun or Moon or zephyr draw aside,
Till the isle's beauty, like a naked bride

---

[20] "a soul within the soul". A possible translation of *epipsychidion*.

[21] "Lucifer". Once the fairest of the angels. "How art thou fallen from heaven, O Lucifer, son of the morning!" (Isaiah 14:12) Lucifer, the rebel or apostate angel, has long been a gay symbol. A gay bar in London is named The Fallen Angel.

Glowing at once with love and loveliness,
Blushes and trembles at its own excess:
Yet, like a buried lamp, a Soul no less
Burns in the heart of this delicious isle,
An atom of th' Eternal, whose own smile
Unfolds itself, and may be felt not seen
O'er the gray rocks, blue waves and forests green,
Filling their bare and void interstices.
But the chief marvel of the wilderness
Is a lone dwelling, built by whom or how
None of the rustic island-people know:
'Tis not a tower of strength, though with its height
It overtops the woods; but, for delight,
Some wise and tender Ocean-King, ere crime
Had been invented, in the world's young prime, [22]
Rear'd it, a wonder of that simple time,
An envy of the isles, a pleasure-house
Made sacred to his sister and his spouse.
It scarce seems now a wreck of human art,
But, as it were, Titanic; in the heart
Of Earth having assum'd its form, then grown
Out of the mountains, from the living stone,
Lifting itself in caverns light and high:
For all the antique and learned imagery
Has been eras'd, and in the place of it
The ivy and the wild-vine interknit

[22] "ere crime / Had been invented..." That is, before a taboo, derived from the *Holiness Code of Leviticus*, made male love into a sin and a crime.

The volumes of their many-twining stems;
Parasite flowers illume with dewy gems
The lampless halls, and when they fade, the sky
Peeps through their winter-woof of tracery
With moonlight patches, or star atoms keen,
Or fragments of the day's intense serene;
Working mosaic on their Parian floors.
And, day and night, aloof, from the high towers
And terraces, the Earth and Ocean seem
To sleep in one another's arms, and dream
Of waves, flowers, clouds, woods, rocks, and all that we
Read in their smiles, and call reality.

This isle and house are mine, and I have vow'd
Thee to be lady of the solitude. [23]
And I have fitted up some chambers there
Looking towards the golden Eastern air,
And level with the living winds, which flow
Like waves above the living waves below.
I have sent books and music there, and all
Those instruments with which high Spirits call
The future from its cradle, and the past
Out of its grave, and make the present last

---

[23] "I have vow'd / Thee to be lady of the solitude." There is a verbal ambiguity here. Either the line means 1) Shelley has vowed that "Emily" will be his "lady of the solitude", or 2) Shelley has vowed that he, himself will be "lady of the solitude" to "Emily" (= Edward). If gender is veiled in *Epipsychidion*, then "lady" could be read as "lord".

In thoughts and joys which sleep, but cannot die,
Folded within their own eternity.
Our simple life wants little, and true taste
Hires not the pale drudge Luxury to waste
The scene it would adorn, and therefore still,
Nature with all her children haunts the hill.
The ring-dove, in the embowering ivy, yet
Keeps up her love-lament, and the owls flit
Round the evening tower, and the young stars glance
Between the quick bats in their twilight dance;
The spotted deer bask in the fresh moonlight
Before our gate, and the slow, silent night
Is measur'd by the pants of their calm sleep.
Be this our home in life, and when years heap
Their wither'd hours, like leaves, on our decay,
Let us become the overhanging day,
The living soul of this Elysian isle,
Conscious, inseparable, one. Meanwhile
We two will rise, and sit, and walk together,
Under the roof of blue Ionian weather,
And wander in the meadows, or ascend
The mossy mountains, where the blue heavens bend
With lightest winds, to touch their paramour;
Or linger, where the pebble-paven shore,
Under the quick, faint kisses of the sea,
Trembles and sparkles as with ecstasy —
Possessing and possess'd by all that is
Within that calm circumference of bliss,

And by each other, till to love and live
Be one: or, at the noontide hour, arrive
Where some old cavern hoar seems yet to keep
The moonlight of the expir'd night asleep,
Through which the awaken'd day can never peep;
A veil for our seclusion, close as night's,
Where secure sleep may kill thine innocent lights;
Sleep, the fresh dew of languid love, the rain
Whose drops quench kisses till they burn again.
And we will talk, until thought's melody
Become too sweet for utterance, and it die
In words, to live again in looks, which dart [24]
With thrilling tone into the voiceless heart,
Harmonizing silence without a sound.
Our breath shall intermix, our bosoms bound,
And our veins beat together; and our lips
With other eloquence than words, eclipse
The soul that burns between them, and the wells
Which boil under our being's inmost cells,
The fountains of our deepest life, shall be
Confus'd in Passion's golden purity,
As mountain-springs under the morning sun.
We shall become the same, we shall be one
Spirit within two frames, oh! wherefore two?

---

[24] "to live again in looks, which dart / With thrilling tone into the voiceless heart." A favorite theme of Shelley's: the eyes as conveyors of love, which he expressed in his poems, in his "Essay on Love", and in *Frankenstein*. (Lauritsen 2007)

One passion in twin-hearts, which grows and grew, [25]
Till like two meteors of expanding flame,
Those spheres instinct with it become the same,
Touch, mingle, are transfigur'd; ever still
Burning, yet ever inconsumable:
In one another's substance finding food,
Like flames too pure and light and unimbu'd
To nourish their bright lives with baser prey,
Which point to Heaven and cannot pass away:
One hope within two wills, one will beneath

---

[25] "We shall become the same, we shall be one / Spirit within two frames." From here until the close of the poem, Shelley describes the union of soul mates, the coming-together of two halves of a primal whole, from the speech of Aristophanes in Plato's Symposium. In Shelley's translation of the *Symposium* (or *Banquet*):

> If Vulcan should stand over the couch of these persons [male lovers] thus affected as they were reclining together, with his tools, and should say to them, "My good people, what is it that you want with one another?" And if, while they were hesitating what to answer, he should proceed to ask, "Do you not desire the closest union and singleness to exist between you, so that you may never be divided night or day? If so, I will melt you together, and make you grow into one, so that both in life and death ye may be undivided. Consider, is this what you desire? Will it content you if you become that which I propose?" We all know that no one would refuse such an offer, but would at once feel that this was what he had ever sought; and intimately to mix and melt and to be melted together with his beloved, so that one should be made out of two. (Shelley 2001)

"One passion in twin-hearts". Compare the the final line of the epitaph that Shelley composed for Edward Williams and himself: "For their two hearts in life were single-hearted." For more on this epitaph: http://paganpressbooks.com/jpl/ASHES.HTM .

Two overshadowing minds, one life, one death,
One Heaven, one Hell, one immortality,
And one annihilation. Woe is me!
The winged words on which my soul would pierce
Into the height of Love's rare Universe,
Are chains of lead around its flight of fire --
I pant, I sink, I tremble, I expire! [26]

****

Passages of the Poem, or Connected Therewith

Here, my dear friend, is a new book for you [27]
I have already dedicated two
To other friends, one female and one male, —
What you are, is a thing that I must veil; [28]
What can this be to those who praise or rail?

---

[26] "I pant, I sink, I tremble, I expire! This is the "death which lovers love" (*Boat on the Serchio*) – orgasm!

[27] In my book, *The Man Who Wrote Frankenstein* (Lauritsen 2007), I argue that Shelley uses "friend" as a code word for the male lover of another man.

[28] "a thing that I must veil." Shelley here indicates that he must veil the person to whom *Epipsychidion* is dedicated. How veil? In the context of these lines – in which female is contrasted to male, mistress to friend – the most plausible interpretation is that Shelley veiled the gender of his friend.

I never was attached to that great sect
Whose doctrine is that each one should select
Out of the world a mistress or a friend,[29]
And all the rest, though fair and wise, commend
To cold oblivion — though 'tis in the code
Of modern morals, and the beaten road[30]
Which those poor slaves with weary footsteps tread
Who travel to their home among the dead
By the broad highway of the world — and so
With one sad friend, and many a jealous foe,
The dreariest and the longest journey go.

Free love has this, different from gold and clay,
That to divide is not to take away.[31]
Like ocean, which the general north wind breaks
Into ten thousand waves, and each one makes
A mirror of the moon — like some great glass,
Which did distort whatever form might pass,

---

[29] "I never was attached to that great sect/ Whose doctrine is that each one should select/ Out of the world a mistress or a friend." In this remarkable passage, Shelley declares both his bisexuality and his allegiance to Free Love, his opposition to obligatory monogamy. Here mistress and friend are presented as counterparts — and as the counterpart of mistress, friend can only be understood in an erotic sense.

[30] "modern morals." That is, Judeo-Christian morals (which condemn male love) as contrasted with the morals of Ancient Greece (which exalted male love). The essence of philosophy of gay liberation

[31] "Free love...." A forthright affirmation of Free Love.

Dashed into fragments by a playful child,
Which then reflects its eyes and forehead mild;
Giving for one, which it could ne'er express,
A thousand images of loveliness.

If I were one whom the loud world held wise,
I should disdain to quote authorities
In commendation of this kind of love: — [32]
Why there is first the God in heaven above,
Who wrote a book called Nature, 'tis to be [33]
Reviewed, I hear, in the next Quarterly;
And Socrates, the Jesus Christ of Greece,
And Jesus Christ Himself, did never cease
To urge all living things to love each other, [34]
And to forgive their mutual faults, and smother
The Devil of disunion in their souls.

I love you! — Listen, O embodied Ray
Of the great Brightness; I must pass away
While you remain, and these light words must be

---

[32] "commendation of this kind of love." In context, what can "this kind of love" refer to, other than male love, or what Shelley might have called "Uranian Love"?

[33] "the God in heaven above, / Who wrote a book called Nature." Here Shelley rebuts the Roman Catholic dogma that sex between males is a sin against nature (*peccatum contra naturam*). Male love is part of nature and therefore cannot be unnatural.

[34] The simplest argument: love is good.

Tokens by which you may remember me.

Start not — the thing you are is unbetrayed,
If you are human, and if but the shade
Of some sublimer spirit....

And as to friend or mistress, 'tis a form;
Perhaps I wish you were one. Some declare
You a familiar spirit, as you are;
Others with a more inhuman
Hint that, though not my wife, you are a woman;
What is the colour of your eyes and hair?
Why, if you were a lady, it were fair [35]
The world should know — but, as I am afraid,
The Quarterly would bait you if betrayed;
And if, as it will be sport to see them stumble
Over all sorts of scandals, hear them mumble
Their litany of curses — some guess right,
And others swear you're a Hermaphrodite; [36]
Like that sweet marble monster of both sexes,
Which looks so sweet and gentle that it vexes
The very soul that the soul is gone
Which lifted from her limbs the veil of stone.

---

[35] "Why, if you were a lady...." The subjunctive implies that Shelley's friend, to whom *Epipsychidion* is covertly dedicated, is male.

[36] "Hermaphrodite". A mythical being that is both male and female. An old code word for a gay person.

. . . .

It is a sweet thing, friendship, a dear balm,
A happy and auspicious bird of calm,
Which rides o'er life's ever tumultuous Ocean;
A God that broods o'er chaos in commotion;
A flower which fresh as Lapland roses are,
Lifts its bold head into the world's frore air,
And blooms most radiantly when others die,
Health, hope, and youth, and brief prosperity;
And with the light and odour of its bloom,
Shining within the dungeon and the tomb; [37]
Whose coming is as light and music are
'Mid dissonance and gloom — a star
Which moves not 'mid the moving heavens alone —
A smile among dark frowns — a gentle tone
Among rude voices, a beloved light,
A solitude, a refuge, a delight.
If I had but a friend! Why, I have three
Even by my own confession; there may be
Some more, for what I know, for 'tis my mind
To call my friends all who are wise and kind, —
And these, Heaven knows, at best are very few;
But none can ever be more dear than you.

---

[37] "Shining within the dungeon and the tomb." These and the preceding lines suggest forbidden love, sexual acts punished by imprisonment and death. During Shelley's entire lifetime, men and boys in England were hanged for having sex with each other.

Why should they be? My muse has lost her wings,
Or like a dying swan who soars and sings,
I should describe you in heroic style,
But as it is, are you not void of guile?

A lovely soul, formed to be blessed and bless:
A well of sealed and secret happiness;
A lute which those whom Love has taught to play
Make music on to cheer the roughest day,
And enchant sadness till it sleeps? ....

. . . .

To the oblivion whither I and thou,
All loving and all lovely, hasten now
With steps, ah, too unequal! may we meet
In one Elysium or one winding-sheet [38]

If any should be curious to discover
Whether to you I am a friend or lover,
Let them read Shakespeare's sonnets, taking thence
A whetstone for their dull intelligence [39]

---

[38] "In one Elysium or one winding-sheet." Shelley's wish that he and his friend be united, in happiness or in death. For a brief essay on this topic: http://paganpressbooks.com/jpl/ASHES.HTM .

[39] In these four lines Shelley discloses that his friend is his lover. Shakespeare's sonnets, which express the love of an older for a younger man, are unmistakably a gay reference. Note Shelley's contempt for the

That tears and will not cut, or let them guess
How Diotima, the wise prophetess,
Instructed the instructor, and why he
Rebuked the infant spirit of melody
On Agathon's sweet lips, which as he spoke
Was as the lovely star when morn has broke
The roof of darkness, in the golden dawn,
Half-hidden, and yet beautiful. [40]
I'll pawn
My hopes of Heaven — you know what they are worth
—
That the presumptuous pedagogues of Earth,
If they could tell the riddle offered here
Would scorn to be, or being to appear
What now they seem and are — but let them chide,
They have few pleasures in the world beside;
Perhaps we should be dull were we not chidden,
Paradise fruits are sweetest when forbidden. [41]
Folly can season Wisdom, Hatred Love.

"dull intelligence" of straight people. G. Wilson Knight (1957) considered these four lines sufficient to identify Shelley as "bisexual".

[40] These seven lines, beginning with "How Diotima ...", refer to Plato's *Symposium*, which Shelley translated in 1818 as *The Banquet*. Male love is at the core of this dialogue; like Shakespeare's sonnets, the *Symposium* has for centuries been used by gay men as a coded reference.

[41] "Paradise fruits are sweetest when forbidden." Again the idea of forbidden love.

. . . .

Farewell, if it can be to say farewell
To those who

. . . .

I will not, as most dedicators do,
Assure myself and all the world and you,
That you are faultless — would to God they were
Who taunt me with your love! I then should wear [42]
These heavy chains of life with a light spirit,
And would to God I were, or even as near it
As you, dear heart. Alas! what are we? Clouds
Driven by the wind in warring multitudes,
Which rain into the bosom of the earth,
And rise again, and in our death and birth,
And through our restless life, take as from heaven
Hues which are not our own, but which are given,
And then withdrawn, and with inconstant glance
Flash from the spirit to the countenance.
There is a Power, a Love, a Joy, a God
Which makes in mortal hearts its brief abode,
A Pythian exhalation, which inspires
Love, only love — a wind which o'er the wires

---

[42] "would to God they were [faultless] / Who taunt me with your love!" Perhaps pure rhetoric; perhaps Shelley actually had been taunted for having a homosexual relationship.

Of the soul's giant harp
There is a mood which language faints beneath;
You feel it striding, as Almighty Death
His bloodless steed....

. . . .

And what is that most brief and bright delight
Which rushes through the touch and through the sight,
And stands before the spirit's inmost throne,
A naked Seraph? None hath ever known.
Its birth is darkness, and its growth desire;
Untameable and fleet and fierce as fire,
Not to be touched but to be felt alone,
It fills the world with glory — and is gone.

. . . .

It floats with rainbow pinions o'er the stream
Of life, which flows, like a dream
Into the light of morning, to the grave
As to an ocean....

. . . .

What is that joy which serene infancy
Perceives not, as the hours content them by,
Each in a chain of blossoms, yet enjoys

The shapes of this new world, in giant toys
Wrought by the busy ever new?
Remembrance borrows Fancy's glass, to show
These forms more sincere
Than now they are, than then, perhaps, they were.
When everything familiar seemed to be
Wonderful, and the immortality
Of this great world, which all things must inherit,
Was felt as one with the awakening spirit,
Unconscious of itself, and of the strange
Distinctions which in its proceeding change
It feels and knows, and mourns as if each were
A desolation....

. . . .

Were it not a sweet refuge, Emily,
For all those exiles from the dull insane [43]
Who vex this pleasant world with pride and pain,
For all that band of sister-spirits known [44]
To one another by a voiceless tone?

. . . .

---

[43] "all those exiles from the dull insane" – Gay men, who are exiles from the stifling and crazy taboos and conventions of normalcy.

[44] "all that band of sister-spirits known / To one another by a voiceless tone." Or brother-spirits. Gay men are able to identify each other by clues to which straight people are insensible; they have *gaydar*.

If day should part us night will mend division
And if sleep parts us — we will meet in vision
And if life parts us — we will mix in death [45]
Yielding our mite [?] of unreluctant breath
Death cannot part us — we must meet again
In all in nothing in delight in pain:
How, why or when or where — it matters not
So that we share an undivided lot....

. . . .

And we will move possessing and possessed

Wherever beauty on the earth's bare [?] breast
Lies like the shadow of thy soul — till we
Become one being with the world we see....

****

[45] "And if life parts us – we will mix in death." Again, Shelley's wish to be united with his lover in death.

APPENDIX VI. The West Portrait of Shelley

The portrait in the frontispiece was painted by William Edward West, an American artist who in 1812 also painted portraits of Byron and his companion, Countess Teresa Guiccioli. The portrait was discovered in 1907 and displayed at a meeting of the Keats-Shelley Memorial Committee in New York City:

> One of the features of the afternoon was the exhibit of a recently discovered portrait of Shelley.... It was painted by William Edward West about two months before the death of the poet. West ... was painting a portrait of Byron. At one of the sittings Shelley visited the studio. West stopped his work to make a sketch of his other poet, from which he later made the painting. (*New York Times*, 15 February 1907)

It was regarded as an authentic portrait of Shelley until Newman Ivey White's biography, *Shelley*, was published in 1940. In a very long and tedious appendix, White impugned the veracity of West and declared that the portrait was not of Shelley, but of Leigh Hunt. White claimed to know exactly where everyone was, what they were doing, and even what they were wearing and thinking, well over a century before; and he thereby deduced that West and Shelley could only have met on a single morning. All that is dubious enough, but White's clincher — that the portrait is really of Leigh Hunt — is blatantly wrong. There are many visual depictions of Hunt, from caricatures to formal portraits — and, despite differences in styles, they all show the same person. Whoever the person in the West portrait may be, he bears no resemblance whatever to Leigh Hunt.

There is no reason to doubt that West was telling the truth. He never attempted to sell the painting and had no motive for lying. I believe intuitively that the man in the portrait is Shelley. Let me explain.

The last major biography of Shelley I read was by Walter Edwin Peck: *Shelley: His Life and Work* (1927). Before this I had read most of Shelley's works, as well as accounts written by people who had actually known him. As soon as I saw the portrait, the frontispiece of Peck's second volume, I had a shock of recognition: *this is Shelley!* I also was struck by the intelligence and beauty of the young man — in his late twenties, as Shelley would have been when West sketched him. To me, he is the Shelley described by Hogg, Trelawny, and Peacock. The man in the portrait is also in accord with the vivid impressions given by two women who knew him. Claire Clairmont wrote the following:

> S——' was beautiful, that kind of beauty which Bacon says is the best — "that which a picture can-

not express." It dwelt upon his countenance, it enshrined his person, and seemed to be a perpetual emanation from himself, rather than any union of exquisite proportions either in form or figure. The beholder saw that he was preeminent in beauty, but could not discover in what that preeminence consisted.... Through all his beauty and splendour, and even through that gay air of careless loveliness which was his usual presence, there peeped slight traces of melancholy and dejection, as if almost unconsciously he were longing for a brighter home than Earth could afford him. (Clairmont)

Byron's companion, Countess Teresa Guiccioli, who was fond of Shelley, wrote:

It was said that in his adolescence he was good-looking — but now he was no longer so. His features were delicate but not regular — except for his mouth which however was not good when he laughed, and was a little spoiled by his teeth, the shape of which was not in keeping with his refinement ... He was also extraordinary in his garb, for he normally wore a jacket like a young college boy's, never any gloves nor polish on his boots — and yet among a thousand he would always have seemed the most finished of gentlemans [sic].... Perhaps never did anyone ever see a man so deficient in beauty who still could produce an impression of it ... It was the fire, the enthusiasm, of his Intelligence that transformed his features. (Tomalin)

Bibliography

Author(s) unknown, *Don Leon: A Poem by Lord Byron ... and Leon to Annabella: An epistle from Lord Byron to Lady Byron,* (first known publication 1866, though probably written in the third or fourth decade of the 19th century), Printed for subscribers by The Fortune Press, London ca. 1934.

Jeremy Bentham, "Offenses Against One's Self: Paederasty." Written ca. 1785 but not published until 1978. Online at: http://paganpressbooks.com/jpl/BENTHAM.HTM .

Sir Richard Burton, "Pederasty" in Section D of "Terminal Essay" in *Arabian Nights,* vol. 10, 1886. Online Burton section with text of essay at: http://paganpressbooks.com/jpl/BURTON.HTM .

Alan Bray, *The Friend,* 2003.

Byron, *Poetical Works,* edited by Frederick Page, 1970.

Andrew Calimach, "Pinning Anal Sex on the Greeks", 2013. Available on the Internet.

Edward Carpenter, *Ioläus: An Anthology of Friendship,* 1906.

—— *My Days. and Dreams: Being Autobiographical Notes,* 1916.

Edward Carpenter and George Barnefield, *The Psychology of the Poet Shelley,* 1925.

Wainwright Churchill, *Homosexual Behavior Among Males: A Cross-Cultural and Cross-Species Investigation,* 1967.

Claire Clairmont, *The Journals of Claire Clairmont,* edited by Marion Kingston Stocking, 1968.

Peter Cochran (editor), *Byron and Women [and men],* 2010. John Lauritsen's review at: http://paganpressbooks.com/jpl/COCHRAN.HTM .

David Crane, *Lord Byron's Jackal: A Life of Edward John Trelawny,* 1999.

Louis Crompton, *Byron and Greek Love: Homophobia in 19th Century England,* 1985.

—— *Homosexuality and Civilization,* 2003.

—— "Don Leon, Byron and Homosexual Law Reform", *Journal of Homosexuality,* 1983.

Stuart Curran, "English Literature: Romanticism" in *Gay and Lesbian Literary Heritage*, edited by Claude J. Summers, 2002.

Gilvanni Dall'Orto, *Tutta un'altra storia: L'omosessualità dall'antichità al secondo dopoguerra*, 2015.

Timothy d'Arch Smith, *Love in Earnest: Some Notes on the Lives and Writings of English 'Uranian' Poets from 1889 to 1930*, 1970.

James Davidson, *The Greeks & Greek Love*, 2007.

Gary Dyer, "Thieves, Boxers, Sodomites, Poets: Being Flash to Byron's Don Juan", PMLA 116.3, pp. 562-578.

Wayne R. Dynes, "Warren Johansson" (Joseph Wallfield), and William A. Percy, *Encyclopedia of Homosexuality*, 1990.

"J.Z. Eglinton" (Walter Breen), *Greek Love*, 1964.

Paul Foot, *Red Shelley*, 1980.

C.S. Ford and F.A. Beach, *Patterns of Sexual Behavior*, 1951.

Benedict Friedlaender, *Die Liebe Platons im Lichte der modernen Biologie*, 1905. Online at: http://paganpressbooks.com/jpl/BENFRIED.HTM .

— *Renaissance des Eros Uranios: Die physiologische Freundschaft, ein normaler Grundtrieb des Menschen und eine Frage der männlichen Gesellungsfreiheit*, 1904.

Count Peter (Pietro) Gamba, *A Narrative of Lord Byron's Last Journey to Greece*, 1825.

Noel I. Garde, *From Jonathan to Gide: The Homosexual in History*, 1964.

Countess Teresa Guiccioli, *My Recollections of Lord Byron and Those of Eye-Witnesses of his Life*, translated from Italian into English by Hubert E. H. Jerningham, 1869.

Kurt Hiller, "Appeal to the Second International Congress for Sexual Reform on Behalf of an Oppressed Human Variety", translated from German by John Lauritsen. Online at: http://paganpressbooks.com/jpl/HILLER.HTM .

Magnus Hirschfeld, *Die Homosexualität des Mannes und des Weibes*, 1914, reprint 1984.

—— *The Homosexuality of Men and Women.* Translated from the German by Michael A. Lombardi-Nash, 2000.

Thomas Jefferson Hogg, *The Life of Percy Bysshe Shelley,* 1858.

Richard Holmes, *Shelley: The Pursuit,* 1974.

"Warren Johansson" and William A. Percy, *Outing: Shattering the Conspiracy of Silence,* 1994.

Frederick L. Jones (editor), *Maria Gisborne & Edward E. Williams: Shelley's Friends: Their Journals and Letters,* 1951.

Selwyn B. Jones, *Shelley Unbound* (unpublished manuscript), 2002.

James Jope, "Interpretation and authenticity of the Lucianic Erotes", *Helios,* Spring 2011.

Alfred Kinsey *et al., Sexual Behavior in the Human Male,* 1948.

—— "Criteria for a hormonal explanation of the homosexual", *Journal of Clinical Endocrinology,* May 1941. Online at: http://paganpressbooks.com/jpl/CRITERIA.HTM .

Wayne Koestenbaum, *Double Talk: The erotics of male literary collaboration,* 1989.

G. Wilson Knight, *Lord Byron's Marriage: The Evidence of Asterisks,* 1957.

—— *The Mutual Flame: On Shakespeare's Sonnets and The Phoenix and the Turtle,* 1955.

John Lauritsen, *A Freethinker's Primer of Male Love,* 1998.

—— *The Man Who Wrote Frankenstein,* 2007.

—— "Down With LGBTQ!", an original Internet article at: http://paganpressbooks.com/jpl/LGBTQ.HTM .

—— "Harriet Shelley", material on Shelley's first wife, 2009.: http://paganpressbooks.com/jpl/HARRIET.HTM .

John Lauritsen and David Thorstad, *The Early Homosexual Rights Movement (1864-1935),* 1974; Revised Second Edition 1995.

"Hans Licht" (Paul Brandt), *Sittengeschichte Griechenlands.* Dresden/Zürich 1925-28. (Bowdlerized English translation, *Sexual Life in Ancient Greece,* London 1932.)

Ernest J. Lovell, Jr; *Captain Medwin: Friend of Byron and Shelley*; 1962.

—— (editor), *Medwin's Conversations of Lord Byron* (originally published 1824) — *Revised with a New Preface by the Author for a New Edition and Annotated by Lady Byron, Sir Charles Napier, John Murray, John Galt, William Harness, Robert Southey, Lady Caroline Lamb, Leigh Hunt, Mary Shelley, E.J. Trelawny, William Fletcher, Countess Teresa Guiccioli, and Others Who Knew the Poet Personally*, 1966.

Lucian, *Erotes*, translated as "Affairs of the Heart" by M.D. Macleod, *Lucian VIII*, Loeb edition, 1967.

Fiona MacCarthy, *Byron: Life and Legend*, 2002.

Leslie A. Marchand, *Byron: A Portrait*, 1970.

H.J. Massingham, *The Friend of Shelley: A Memoir of Edward John Trelawny*, 1930.

"Xavier Mayne" (pseudonym of Edward Irenaeus Prime-Stevenson), *The Intersexes: A History of Similisexualism as a Problem in Social Life*, privately printed with Preface dated 1908, reprint 1975.

Thomas Medwin, *The Life of Percy Bysshe Shelley*, 1847; New, expanded edition edited by H. Buxton Forman, 1913.

—— *Oswald and Edwin, Sketches in Hindoostan, Ahasulerus;* Introduction for Garland edition by Donald H. Reiman, 1978 (original publications 1820-1823).

Doris Langley Moore, *The Late Lord Byron: Posthumous Dramas*, 1961.

—— *Lord Byron: Accounts Rendered*, 1974.

Rictor Norton, *Mother Clap's Molly House: The Gay Subculture in England, 1700-1830*, 1992.

—— *Myth of the Modern Homosexual*, 1997.

James A. Notopoulos, *The Platonism of Shelley*, 1949.

Iris Origo, *The Last Attachment: The Story of Byron and Teresa Guiccioli*, 1949.

Thomas Love Peacock, *Memoirs of Percy Bysshe Shelley*, 1858-1862.

—— *Rhododaphne*, 1818.

William A. Percy and Warren Johansson, *Pederasty and Pedagogy in Archaic Greece*, 1995.

"Numa Praetorius" (Eugen Wilhelm), "*Die strafrechtlichen Bestimmungen gegen dem gleichgeschlechtlichen Verkehr historisch und kritisch dargestellt*". *Jahrbuch für sexuelle Zwischenstufen unter besonderer Berücksichtigung der Homosexualität, wissenschaftlich-humanitären Comitée*. Volume I, pp. 97-158. Berlin 1899. Online at: http://paganpressbooks.com/jpl/NUMA.HTM .

William St. Clair, *The Godwins and the Shelleys: A biography of a family*, 1989.

— *Trelawny: The incurable romancer*. 1977.

Scott, Walter Sidney (editor), *The Athenians — Being correspondence between Thomas Jefferson Hogg and his friends Thomas Love Peacock, Leigh Hunt, Percy Bysshe Shelley, and others*, Golden Cockerel Press, limited edition of 350 copies, 1943.

Percy Bysshe Shelley, *Poetical Works*, edited by Thomas Hutchinson; a new edition, corrected by G.M. Matthews), 1970.

—— *The Complete Poetry of Percy Bysshe Shelley,* edited by Donald H. Reiman and Neil Fraistat, 3 volumes, 2000-2012

Mary Wollstonecraft Shelley (attributed to), James Rieger (editor), *Frankenstein or, The Modern Prometheus: The 1818 Text,* 1974.

Robert Metcalf Smith, *The Shelley Legend,* 1945.

Emily W. Sunstein, *Mary Shelley: Romance and Reality,* 1989.

Alistair Sutherland and Patrick Anderson, *Eros: An Anthology of Male Friendship,* 1963.

John Addington Symonds, *The Memoirs of John Addington Symonds: The Secret Homosexual Life of a Leading Nineteenth-Century Man of Letters,* P. Grosskurth (editor), 1984.

—— *A Problem in Greek Ethics,* 1883. Online in Rictor Norton's website.

.

—— *Shelley,* 1887.

Lionel Tiger, *Men in Groups,* 1969.

Robert Deam Tobin, *Peripheral Desires: The German Discovery of Sex,* 2015. John Lauritsen's review at: http://paganpressbooks.com/jpl/TOBIN.HTM .

Claire Tomalin, *Shelley and his World*, 1980.

Edward John Trelawny, *Adventures of a Younger Son*, 1831. Unexpurgated edition edited by William St. Clair, 1974.

—— *Recollections of Shelley and Byron*, 1858.

—— *Records of Shelley, Byron, and the Author*, 1878.

C.A. Tripp, review of *Sexual Preference: Its development in men and women* (vol. 1), *Sexual Preference: Statistical appendix* (vol. 2) Online at: http://paganpressbooks.com/jpl/TRIPP.HTM .

Thorkil Vangaard, *Phallós: A Symbol and its History in the Male World*, 1972.

Beert C. Verstraete and Vernon Provencal (editors), *Same-Sex Desire and Love in Greco-Roman Antiquity and in The Classical Tradition of the West*, 2005.

Elisar Von Kupffer, *Lieblingminne und Freundesliebe in der Weltliteratur*, 1900.

Jack Gumpert Wasserman, "Homosexuality in Venice in the time of Lord Byron", in Cochran, *op. cit.*

Timothy Webb, *The violet in the crucible: Shelley and translation,* 1976.

James D. Weinrich, "Nonreproduction, homosexuality, transsexualism, and intelligence: I. A systematic literature review", *Journal of Homosexuality,* Spring 1978.

Craig A. Williams, *Roman Homosexuality: Ideologies of Masculinity in Classical Antiquity,* 1999.

Ian Young, *The Male Homosexual in Literature,* 1982.

Phyllis Zimmerman, *Shelley's Fiction,* 1998.

The author

John Lauritsen studied English Literature and Social Relations at Harvard. Before retirement he made his living as a market research analyst, while writing on the side. In 1982 he founded Pagan Press. As author, co-author, or editor, he now has a dozen books to his credit. He is best known for his writings on Gay Liberation, AIDS criticism, and the English Romantics. These have been widely translated. He lives in a Victorian house in Dorchester, Massachusetts. His personal website is: http://paganpressbooks.com/jpl .

The cover

The drawing of Edward John Trelawny was done by Semour Kirkup.

The typefaces

Golden Cockerel is used for the text. Designed by Eric Gill in 1929-1931 for the Golden Cockerel Press, the typeface reflects his skill as a sculptor, engraver, and calligrapher. In accordance with Gill's sentiments ("The Procrustean Bed" , *An Essay on Typography*, 1936), the right-hand margins in this book are not justified.

The front cover typeface is Zapf Humanist.

Ganymede with Zeus as an eagle
Sculpture by Bertel Thorvaldsen